REREADING LITERATURE
Blake

William Blake

Edward Larrissy

Basil Blackwell

© Edward Larrissy 1985

First published 1985

Basil Blackwell Ltd
108 Cowley Road, Oxford OX4 1JF, UK

Basil Blackwell Inc.
432 Park Avenue South, Suite 1505,
New York, NY 10016, USA

British Library Cataloguing in Publication Data

Larrissy, Edward
    William Blake. – (Rereading Literature)
    1. Blake, William, *1757–1827* – Criticism and interpretation
    I. Title   II. Series
    821'.7   PR4147

ISBN 0-631-13485-9
ISBN 0-631-13504-9 Pbk

Library of Congress Cataloging in Publication Data
Larrissy, Edward
    William Blake. – (Rereading Literature)
    Includes index.
    1. Blake, William, *1757–1827* – Criticism and interpretation
    I. Title   II. Series: Rereading literature
    PR4147.L37   1985   821'.7   85–9105

ISBN 0-631-13485-9
ISBN 0-631-13504-9 (pbk.)

Typeset by Cambrian Typesetters, Frimley, Surrey
Printed in Great Britain by Whitstable Litho Ltd, Kent

Contents

To Jocelyn Larrissy

Editor's Preface

Blake is England's greatest revolutionary artist, and it is therefore not wholly mischievous to ask why he has met with such widespread acclaim from a critical orthodoxy hardly revolutionary in its interests. Several answers suggest themselves, beyond the obvious fact that dead revolutionaries are a good deal more acceptable than living ones. It is not always easy to know exactly what he is saying; his political vision often assumes the shape of a timeless drama of energy and repression, which is rather more palatable to liberal humanist taste than talk of popular insurrection; and the critical acclaim has in any case been far from universal, relegating as it has sometimes done the more overtly revolutionary writings as turgid obscurantism, and retrieving a few songs more susceptible of New Critical treatment. Blake's richness of ambiguity, in short, has tended to redeem his poetry for those who find any more didactic political intent incompatible with the 'literary'.

Part of the originality of Edward Larrissy's study lies in its subtle awareness of the *relationship* between Blake's symbolic ambiguity and his strenuous political engagement, aspects of his work sometimes seen as antithetical. To be effective, revolutionary desire for Blake must achieve its appropriate artistic and institutional forms; but in order to remain faithful to itself it must also cast a distancing ironic eye upon all such forms, which will always be something less than the energies they contain. So it is, as Larrissy demonstrates, that form in Blake is always at once limiting and liberatory – just as energy and enslavement, law and desire, come to figure in his work as mutual conditions of one another. A way of putting this point, then, is to claim that Blake's poetry throws into question the false distinction, common to our own time, between a monolithic political commitment on the one hand, and an endless ironic open-mindedness (whether New Critical or deconstructive) on the other.

Without in the least denigrating the mystical or esoteric Blake – who is not, after all, easily separable from the political one – Larrissy shows just what an astonishingly thoroughgoing radical Blake is, alert to the interlockings of class and sexual oppression, steeped in the radical Protestant tradition, surprisingly modern in his subtle view of ideology and deeply at one with the viewpoint of the emergent working class of nineteenth-century England. In all of this, there is no doubt that he is of the devil's party, and knows it. Yet without relinquishing anything of the force of such a politics, Blake is painfully conscious of how it must be articulated in the idioms and conventions of a given, limited history – and it is from this double vision, Larrissy claims, that his famous duplicities and ambiguities arise. Prizing the 'original', he is forced to be an inveterate parodist of others' works; valuing a pure, primordial voice, he 'grafts' and splices different discourses together; deeply serious about innocence and utopian joy, he draws sardonic attention to the limited forms or enclosures within which alone such innocence can thrive. Denouncing injustice and oppression, he veers ironically around to scrutinize the credentials of the very voices which deliver such denunciations.

In all of these ways, Blake's poetry undermines the authoritarianism of a single meaning, and so begins to transfigure our habits of reading. Larrissy offers us a Blake who, like Brecht in our own time, is beyond both political dogmatism and liberal scepticism, and through whose work we may therefore begin to explore the significance of that far less familiar, more unsettling stance we may term revolutionary ambiguity.

Terry Eagleton

Acknowledgements

Parts of this book, in slightly different versions, appeared in *Red Letters*, no. 8 (1978), and in *1789: Reading Writing Revolution*, Proceedings of the 1981 Essex Conference on the Sociology of Literature, ed. Francis Barker et al. (Colchester, 1982).

I should like to thank the many friends and acquaintances who have discussed this work with me. In particular I am grateful to John Beer, with whom I began my studies on Blake; and to Terry Eagleton, to whom I owe an incalculable debt. I am also indebted, for specific suggestions and illuminating remarks, to Richard Ellmann, Andrew Lincoln, Julian Rees and my editor at Blackwell, Philip Carpenter. It scarcely needs saying that none of these people is responsible for the errors and eccentricities to be found in this work.

I am grateful for the accurate typing of Janet Bailey, secretary of the Department of Classical Civilization, University of Warwick.

The author and publisher are grateful to the Fitzwilliam Museum, Cambridge for permission to reproduce the following illustrations by William Blake: 'The Lamb' (from *Songs of Innocence*) and 'Infant Sorrow' (from *Songs of Experience*).

Textual Note and Abbreviations

The text of Blake used is that in *The Complete Poetry and Prose of William Blake*, ed. David V. Erdman, commentary by Harold Bloom (Berkeley and Los Angeles, University of California Press, 1982) referred to as E. This is a newly revised version of *The Poetry and Prose of William Blake*, also edited by Erdman, and published in 1965 by Doubleday, New York, with different pagination. I also give reference to *The Complete Writings of William Blake*, ed. Geoffrey Keynes (London, Oxford University Press, 1972), referred to as K.

Other abbreviations used are:

IB *The Illuminated Blake*, annotated by David V. Erdman (London, Oxford University Press, 1975)

MHH The Marriage of Heaven and Hell

References to Blake's text give plate or page number, followed by a colon, followed by line number.

1 William Blake and
Songs of Innocence

William Blake (1757–1827) was not on the side of the angels. The son of a hosier, he was brought up in a time when such small tradesmen tended to be radicals. Unlike so many other well-known poets of his day, he did not receive a formal liberal education. He went to a drawing-school at the age of ten or eleven, the only school he ever attended. At the age of fourteen he was apprenticed to an engraver, and at the age of twenty-one he became a student at the Royal Academy. From about this time he began to follow the profession in which he would be occupied, with only intermittent success, for the rest of his life: that of a commercial engraver of illustrations and designs for books. Unlike so many poets in the canon until quite recent times, he had to work for a living.

Blake was nineteen at the time of the American Declaration of Independence, and sympathized with the American revolutionaries, as he was to do with the French revolutionaries thirteen years later. It seems probable, too, that his family had some connection with whatever was left of those eccentric-sounding radical Protestant sects, such as the Ranters and the Muggle-tonians, founded in the period of the English Revolution, over a century before. Of course, his profession brought him into contact with fashionable liberal and Romantic ideas, many of which were congenial enough to somebody from his background. But that background also made his response to them quite complex, and he always remained to some extent an outsider with regard even to the liberal ideas of his own time. The complexity of his inheritance seems to have contributed to a curious anxiety about his ability to convey his ideas without the taint of influences which might detract from their purity. This anxiety may seem odd in one whose work is so revolutionary in both method and message. For Blake wasn't just an outsider: he was a violent and acutely perceptive opponent.

Like so many of his radical contemporaries he railed against the injustices of 'Priest & King', but there are few of his contemporaries who felt so keenly the fact that, as William Godwin said, 'the spirit and character of the government intrude themselves into every rank of society' (*Caleb Williams*, Preface to 2nd edn). But part of Blake's power is that he is not so certain as Godwin that this is a matter of 'intrusion': Blake seems, indeed, to have felt that a tyrant on the throne implied a tyrant at the head of the breakfast table. But he was by no means certain that domestic forms of oppression had simply resulted from the influence of unnatural political depotism. Perhaps both resulted from some far-off catastrophe. Many of Blake's poems are criticisms of oppressive uses of power on many levels, and they imply that there is a link between the use of power when one individual belittles another and the use of power on a large political and economic scale:

> Pity would be no more,
> If we did not make somebody Poor:
> And Mercy no more could be,
> If all were as happy as we
> ('The Human Abstract', E27/K217)

These lines could mean, 'To pity people is to impoverish and belittle them: the two acts are simultaneous.' Or they could mean, 'We may feel complacent about the fact that economic poverty allows us to feel pity and mercy.' Somebody who could write these lines would have to be either a pessimist or a very thorough-going revolutionary.

It is an index of the energy of Blake's thought that he was the latter. For while he saw the evils of society as deep-seated, and not to be cured by the deposing of a few kings, he did believe that those evils were worth taking on.

This belief permitted him to become the greatest radical poet in English. For he was able to castigate a social system, criticize hypocrisy and analyse psychological repression at one and the same time. His description of the Industrial Revolution is full of bitterness at the alienation of labour:

> And all the arts of life they changd into the arts of death
> The hour glass contemnd because its simple workmanship
> Was as the workmanship of the plowman & the water wheel
> That raises water into Cisterns broken & burnd in fire
> Because its workmanship was like the workmanship of the Shepherd
> And in their stead intricate wheels invented Wheel without wheel
> To perplex youth in their outgoings & to bind to labours
> Of day & night the myriads of Eternity. that they might file
> And polish brass & iron hour after hour laborious workmanship
> Kept ignorant of the use that they might spend the days of wisdom
> In sorrowful drudgery to obtain a scanty pittance of bread
> In ignorance to view a small portion & think that All
> And call it Demonstration blind to all the simple rules of life
>
> (*The Four Zoas*, 92:21–33, E364/K337)

It is typical of Blake, however, that he should link the fact of an oppressive economic system with that of the oppression of women:

With what sense does the parson claim the labour of
    the farmer?
What are his nets & gins & traps. & how does he
    surround him
With cold floods of abstraction, and with forests of
    solitude,
To build him castles and high spires. where kings &
    priests may dwell.
Till she who burns with youth. and knows no fixed lot;
    is bound
In spells of law to one she loaths: and must she drag
    the chain
Of life, in weary lust! must chilling murderous
    thoughts. obscure
The clear heaven of her eternal spring? to bear the
    wintry rage
Of a harsh terror driv'n to madness, bound to hold a
    rod
Over her shrinking shoulders all the day; & all the
    night
To turn the wheel of false desire: and longings that
    wake her womb
To the abhorred birth of cherubs in the human form
That live a pestilence & die a meteor & are no more.
(*Visions of the Daughter's of Albion*, 5:17–29, E49/K193)

The transition from the parson to the youthful woman is
direct, and establishes a clear causal link: 'To build him
castles and high spires. where kings & priests may dwell. /
Till she who burns with youth ... is bound ...' But
Blake's insight would not be so profound if it were not for
his clear sense that human beings are constrained by
ideologies and projections which, as individuals, they are
not responsible for, and which may run counter to their
interests and desires. In the same poem, *Visions of the
Daughters of Albion*, the maiden Oothoon loves Theotormon,
but when he discovers that she has been raped by Bromion
(probably a slave-owner) he sits 'wearing the threshold

hard / With secret tears' (2:6–7) and turns away from Oothoon. He in himself is not the source of the ideology of purity and intactness: that derives from the tyrant–god Urizen:

> O Urizen! Creator of men! mistaken Demon of
>   heaven:
> Thy joys are tears! thy labour vain, to form men in
>   thine image.
> How can one joy absorb another? are not different joys
> Holy, eternal, infinite! and each joy is a Love.
> (Visions, 5:3–6, E48/K192)

Furthermore, even if one were to admit the validity of that ideology, Theotormon's response would still seem completely disproportionate, for Oothoon submitted to Bromion against her will. Theotormon is the victim of a type of false consciousness.

It's not much use trying to see Blake as a precursor of historical materialism: he doesn't allow that the economic mode of production determines consciousness. But he does have a conception, startlingly original in his time, of how modes of production, modes of consciousness and cultural institutions may be intimately related. And in fact he does possess one important point in common with Marxist thought. That is, he is a sympathizer with the liberal thinking of the late eighteenth century who is nevertheless acutely conscious of the limitations of that thinking from the standpoint of a communitarian social ideal. In particular, he implicitly repudiates the optimistic, liberal, Enlightenment talk about 'equality before the law' and 'universal toleration', for he seems to have some notion that such talk is based on a facile and unhistorical assumption that all human beings are alike: 'How can the giver of gifts experience the delights of the merchant . . . How different their eye and ear! how different the world to them!' (5:12, 16) He attributes the Enlightenment obsession with sameness, with identity, to Urizen, the tyrant–god, thus suggesting that in his time tyrants and liberators have a certain amount in common. And he uses economic examples, as we have seen, to illustrate the fact of differences between individuals, revealing that the talk of equality, freedom and toleration is a mask for the cruel whims of the market.

So Blake is not on the side of the angels. And yet his firm insistence in *The Marriage of Heaven and Hell* that he is of the Devil's party may seem a trifle too loud, especially since he stresses that opposing points of view ('contraries') will always exist and are necessary to each other. We will suggest that Blake's firmness is meant to conceal what it in fact reveals: a fear that all firmness, like all definite form, is limiting because it excludes other possible views or forms. This fear is balanced against the suspicion that without firmness, without form – in fact without limitation and exclusion – no expression would be possible. These two points of view comprise an ambivalence about form and the means of expression which appears throughout Blake's work.

Certain key words, for instance, constantly carry the weight of this ambivalence. 'Bound', as we shall see, is one. Another is 'state'. On the title page to the volume *Songs of Innocence and of Experience* (1794) there is a sub-title: *Shewing the Two Contrary States of the Human Soul*. We know what the names of the states are: 'Innocence' and 'Experience'. But we may miss the implication that the states of the human soul are only two in number: when you have passed through innocence and experience there are no more states to go through. This makes a state seem a rare thing: a class with only two members. Clearly a state is a condition of the soul, or a set of dispositions. And yet it sounds curiously static, rigid or confining, especially since it exists in only two forms.

And why are the states said to be 'contrary'? 'Opposite' would seem to be an obvious synonym. But in what sense can states of the soul be said to be 'opposite'? Presumably in the sense that all the values held in one are negated in the other, and replaced by opposing ones. But which values are thought to be opposites is a question determined by cultural presuppositions. Though anybody can understand the broad sense in which 'love' and 'hate' are opposites, the ramified social expressions they take may differ widely from culture to culture. 'Innocence' and 'Experience' are here set up as opposites, and this may seem an obvious idea. But we should not assume, on the basis of our own use of the words, that we know exactly how Blake is using them. On the other hand it seems clear from the most cusory reading that the identity of each term is defined in relation to the other.

Does this mean that the terms are dialectical? It's by no means clear from the 1794 volume that Blake thought so: there the two states seem fixed in isolation from each other by the structure of the book, even if one soon discovers that they have some elements in common. But as it happens we know more about contraries from *The Marriage of Heaven and Hell*, and it's clear from this that Blake could think of them as dialectical in more than a loose sense: they continually produced syntheses: 'Without Contraries is no progression. Attraction and Repulsion, Reason and Energy, Love and Hate, are necessary to Human existence' (pl. 3, E34/K149).

The idea of progression implies that one may stand outside a pair of contraries – for example, if one has experienced their operation, and then the consequent progress – and say, as it were, 'I have been through them. Each was limited (because not affording a comprehensive view) but each was necessary to bring me to where I am now.'

And indeed Blake does thus suggest the possibility of an objective, impartial view of contraries:

The Giants who formed this world into its sensual existence and now seem to live in it in chains; are in truth. the causes of its life & the sources of all activity, but the chains are, the cunning of weak and tame minds. which have power to resist energy. according to the proverb, the weak in courage is strong in cunning.

> Thus one portion of being, is the Prolific. the other, the Devouring: to the devourer it seems as if the producer was in his chains, but it is not so, he only takes portions of existence and fancies that the whole.
>
> But the Prolific would cease to be Prolific unless the Devourer as a sea received the excess of his delights . . .
>
> These two classes of men are always upon earth, & they should be enemies; whoever tries to reconcile them seeks to destroy existence.
>
> (pls 16–17, E40/K155)

On a cursory reading this might seem very firm for warfare. After all, from a reading of the whole of *The Marriage* it's clear that Blake presents himself (or the represented speaker) as being, like Milton, 'of the Devil's party'. But it's a very philosophical type of warrior who is not only aware of the necessity of the enemy, but regards his own existence as constituted by them. On the other hand it remains true that *The Marriage* is provocatively and combatively written from what purports to be the Satanic point of view. When Devourers are given a say (which isn't often) their arguments are rejected. One such Devourer is the Angel who objects to one of Blake's visions: 'thy phantasy has imposed upon me & thou oughtest to be ashamed' (pl. 20, E42/K157). But Blake replies, 'we impose on one another, & it is but lost time to converse with you whose works are only Analytics'. In other words, the Angel believes in immutable objective truth. But Blake seems to think that truth is only to be found in the partial and interested visions of particular human beings: 'God only Acts & Is, in existing beings or Men' (pl. 16, E40/K155). Except that, as we have seen, he is aware of the possibility of some kind of relatively objective stance from which one may concede the necessity of one's opponent.

Perhaps we have seen enough to suggest that Blake is, as it were, wishing himself into a more firmly Satanic position than he is in fact content with: he tries to sound partial and detached at the same time. The idea of 'imposition' would support this: it sounds reminiscent of the tyrannical Urizen. Yet the phrase 'we impose on one another' implies that 'imposition' is a feature of all discourse including Blake's. In the context of Blake's other works the word rings with an ambivalent and troubled note. It occurs elsewhere in *The Marriage*: 'The Prophets Isaiah and Ezekiel dined with me, and I asked them how they dared so roundly to assert. that God spake to them; and whether they did not think at the time, that they would be misunderstood, & so be the cause of *imposition*' (pl. 12, E38/K153; emphasis added). In the ensuing conversation Isaiah says, 'In ages of imagination this firm perswasion removed mountains; but many are not capable of a firm perswasion of any thing.' Is Blake pressing himself into a 'firm perswasion' in *The Marriage*?'

II

To return to the *Songs*: the term 'state', like 'imposition' and 'firm perswasion', can suggest both energetic express- iveness and rigid limitation. But can the apparently benign state of Innocence be limiting?

The illuminations to *Songs of Innocence* tend to have certain characteristics in common: 'Blake is quick to establish his key visual motifs: enclosed settings – whether composed of naturalistic trees, shrubs or vines, as on the frontispiece; or more abstract, decorative vegetation, as on the 'Introduction' plate – invariably frame words or visual scenes which express a secure, unthreatened innocence.'[1] The borders are, however, borders: they frame and enclose. There is a neatness about *Songs of Innocence* (and *Experience*) which is sometimes lacking in his other illuminated works. The illuminations enforce the idea of a 'state' both by expressing it and by, quite clearly, delimiting it. It may seem curious that this should be true of *Innocence*. But, as Anne Mellor well says, 'Both the prosody and the illustrations of these songs emphasize the closed, completed nature of Blake's world of Innocence . . . [the] conception of an enclosed world under the protection of a kindly guardian or benevolent deity is reinforced by the consistently tectonic constructions and framed forms of these designs.'[2] Mellor mentions prosody as well as illustrations. Her argument comes close to invoking the suspect notion that regularity and repetition in poems are marks of contraint. If this were so then most hymns, ballads, folksongs and nursery rhymes could be seen as formally 'closed-in' in a way that suggested 'an enclosed world'. Furthermore, it's possible to confuse these notions with the idea of metrical regularity – which Blake's *Songs* don't strictly possess. Indeed, in this combination of insistent repetition with metrical freedom one may see another mark of Blake's paradox of freedom within limitation.

That there is regularity as well as repetition is not in doubt:

> Little Lamb I'll tell thee,
> Little Lamb I'll tell thee!
> He is called by thy name,
> For he calls himself a Lamb:
> He is meek & he is mild,
> He became a little child:
> I a child & thou a Lamb,
> We are called by his name.
> Little Lamb God bless thee.
> Little Lamb God bless thee.
>
> ('The Lamb'; see figure 1)

This must be the best-known of the Songs of Innocence. But 'fearful symmetry' ('The Tyger') is associated with *Songs of Experience*. Roman Jakobson, in a highly technical, but very acute and illuminating essay, refers to the 'eloquent' and 'stunning' symmetry of the verbal art of 'Infant Sorrow' from *Experience*, relating this to the 'geometrical' quality of its illumination (figure 2).[3] It is easy to see how such qualities strengthen the idea of the 'swadling bands' in the poem, and the bonds of *Experience* in general.

Figure 1 'The Lamb', *Songs of Innocence*

But in fact it is also true that *Songs of Innocence* possess every stylistic point by virtue of which one feels that *Experience* is geometrical and symmetrical. Yet as we shall see this is undoubtedly the case. It is only because of the leafiness of the frames that one feels they may be benign. But frames they are. And the poems are full of insistent repetition.

Figure 2   'Infant Sorrow', *Songs of Experience*

Of course, it is wrong to pluck supposedly autonomous 'stylistic features' out of context. The speaker and sentiments of 'The Lamb' are clearly different from those of *Experience* poems, and thus our understanding of the function of parallelisms and repetition will be different for each series. But how different? It doesn't take long for most readers to feel that *Innocence* is not the happy land they hoped for. And, if the tone is not entirely happy, perhaps there is something to be said for the idea that the verbal art of *Innocence* expresses a degree of enclosure. In *Experience* the symmetry of the verbal art reinforces the stark rigidity of the designs, as Jakobson shows. In *Innocence* the refrains, repetitions and parallelisms, though apparently benign in content, could be seen as constricting when taken with the neat frames for the designs, though these are also benignly leafy and springlike. If there is a case, it would be for an insufferable or suffocating benignity. But this must rest on more detailed analysis.

III

'The Chimney Sweeper' is one of those Songs of Innocence that instantly trouble the reader who expects only harmlessness from them:

> When my mother died I was very young,
> And my father sold me while yet my tongue,
> Could scarcely cry weep weep weep weep.
> So your chimneys I sweep & in soot I sleep.
>
> Theres little Tom Dacre who cried when his head
> That curl'd like a lambs back, was shav'd, so I said.
> Hush Tom never mind it, for when your head's bare,
> You know that the soot cannot spoil your white hair.
>
> And so he was quiet, & that very night,
> As Tom was a sleeping he had such a sight,
> That thousands of sweepers Dick, Joe, Ned & Jack
> Were all of them lock'd up in coffins of black,
>
> And by came an Angel who had a bright key,
> And he open'd the coffins & set them all free.
> Then down a green plain leaping laughing they run
> And wash in a river and shine in the Sun.
>
> Then naked & white, all their bags left behind,
> They rise upon clouds, and sport in the wind.
> And the Angel told Tom if he'd be a good boy,
> He'd have God for his father & never want joy.

And so Tom awoke and we rose in the dark
And got with our bags & our brushes to work.
Tho' the morning was cold, Tom was happy & warm,
So if all do their duty, they need not fear harm.

(E10/K117–18)

The last line has a deadly force – unless one is concerned to preclude all irony from *Innocence*. But can one do this? A reading of *Songs of Experience* and, indeed, anything more than a cursory reading of Blake, suggests that the last line is a vicious parody of sentiments which, though they may be read as sincerely held by the little chimney sweep, are the result of indoctrination by religiose hypocrites. But we can perhaps try to take the poem on its own, and divorce it from all Blake's other works. Or we can read it only in conjunction with other *Innocence* poems, because they were written at more or less the same time and are thus clear guides to his intention at the time of writing. The latter course is taken by E.D. Hirsch, Jr, in discussing this very poem:

> If we try to deduce Blake's 'system' or his original intentions from the way we read his *Songs* [*Innocence and Experience*], we are arguing in a circle. We are saying for example, that Blake must have intended to write a sequel because the *Songs of Innocence* are ironical, and that the *Songs of Innocence* are ironical because Blake always intended to compose a sequel.[4]

Hirsch proposes that we should isolate a particular time in Blake's life and identify his intention from that. The underlying assumption is that intention speaks with one voice. The effect is to make works of art seem monolithic and one-dimensional. In opposition to this view, we shall assume that human beings are so constituted that their intentions may be diverse, even in one action; that unconscious and unintended desires and feelings may express themselves alongside intentions; and that access to intention is uncertain, if it is taken to mean something prior to the actual composition of the poem.

In any case, Hirsch's argument suffers from a more basic infirmity: if we were to be really serious and thorough in our attempt to isolate the original intention, we should have to exclude even the other Songs of Innocence from consideration of 'The Chimney Sweeper'. For the other songs could not possibly have been written simultaneously. (As it happens they were written over a number of years.) But nobody in fact reads, or is capable of reading, in this way. We can only read a poem because we have had experience of trying to make sense of poetic convention when reading other poems: to put it in structuralist terms, this is how we learn to *motivate* poetic devices. Furthermore, all readers will bring more or less knowledge about what is signified in a text (the 'content'). And if they feel ignorant they may try to find out more.

If we feel ignorant faced with 'The Chimney Sweeper' we might do one or both of two things: read more Blake; or try to find out more about the practice of sending young children up chimneys to clean them in the eighteenth century. Anybody who tries to stop the reader doing this is attempting to fix the meaning of the poem and make it a function of the supposed immediate *presence* of meaning. But meaning is never present in the sense of being an isolated, instantaneous act unrelated to any other such act. It is always differential: defined by the way its signs differ from or resemble other signs. In fact, to find out the meaning of any sign we have to do precisely what Hirsch fears: argue 'in a circle'. The most obvious illustration of this fact is the use of a dictionary, where when you look up one word you are given another as its meaning, and when you look up that, yet another; and so *ad infinitum*. It is because of the notion of presence that Hirsch is so anxious to establish the times at which different phases of Blake's development are supposed to have occurred, and especially to make those phases a means of restricting unruly meanings, such as irony which is difficult to assimilate.

But we shall turn shamelessly to *Songs of Experience*. There we find another poem called 'The Chimney Sweeper', which gives a clearly disillusioned view of this type of exploitation. The very least you could deduce from this is that Blake was always potentially somebody who could condemn chimney-sweeping. Let us make an assumption: there is irony in the *Innocence* 'Chimney Sweeper'. Indeed, Hirsch would admit as much: he merely wishes to play down its role and assert that the essence of the poem is innocent joy. But this is an evasion of its disturbing complexity.

IV

The irony of 'The Chimney Sweeper' can be better understood if one looks at the way it draws on traditions which include hymns and improving songs for children and workers. The platitudinous moral of the last line is particularly familiar from this tradition. Isaac Watts's *Divine Songs for Children* are often mentioned as antecedents of *Songs of Innocence*. And that great hymnographer's works are certainly marked by the air and diction of conscious moral improvement:

> Happy the child whose tender years
> 　Receive instructions well;
> Who hates the sinner's path, and fears
> 　The road that leads to hell.[5]

Blake's 'Chimney Sweeper' is, however, not so close to such *Divine Songs*, with their abstract moralizing, as to the *Moral Songs*, probably added in 1740.[6] Here, as in Blake's poem, a small dramatic scene is created, and a moral drawn. Thus, in 'The Sluggard', the decline of a lazy person is noted, and the lesson is:

> That man's but a picture of what I might be.
> But thanks to my friends for their care in my breeding,
> Who taught me betimes to love working and reading.[7]

Consider also 'The Beggar's Petition' by Thomas Moss

(but often added to *Divine Songs* after about 1787).[8] The beggar asks for relief in the last line: 'Oh! give relief, and heaven will bless your store.'[9]

But the situation of such children is abstract: Blake is more specific: he writes about chimney sweepers and charity-school children. And, if as children they are helpless, they are still more helpless as the particular children they happen to be. If 'The Chimney Sweeper' were read without irony it would not merely seem like any improving hymn: it would seem to be one that enjoined passive acceptance of exploitation, offering religion as opiate.

And such songs and hymns were written. Paul Fauvet shows how the poems of the Evangelical Hannah More characteristically 'take the form of a confrontation between a "bad", misguided workman who doubts the wisdom of Providence, or is attracted to radical ideas and a "good" character who is a God-fearing defender of the status quo'.[10] He gives as an example the political ballad 'The Riot, or Half a Loaf is Better than No Bread', written during the food riots of 1795. Tom Hod argues for a riot because he is hungry. But Jack Anvil speaks for moderation, 'saying that God blesses England', and pointing out that they are 'squandering time and money' (Fauvet's words):

> Let us remember whenever we meet
> The more ale we drink, boys, the less we shall eat.
> On those days spent in riot, no bread you brought
>   home,
> Had you spent them in labour you must have had
>   some.[11]

The purpose of such propaganda was, as Fauvet says, the 'ideological assimilation of the new working-class':

> the early industrial revolution posed certain problems
> of an ideological nature – in particular the necessity
> for a new work-discipline, dictated not by the rhythm
> of the seasons, but by that of the machine. It was

therefore imperative that the new workforce be integrated into the dominant ideology – or, to use the
language of the time, that they should be 'Godly'.[12]

It's a bit sweeping to reduce the dominant ideology, or its
requirements, to 'godliness', since the latter took many
forms, and the former exacted much more than religious
observance, and was, in any case, marked by internal
contradiction. But as a rough description of Hannah
More's purpose this will serve. The trouble is that Blake's
Songs of Innocence date from before the 1790s, when Hannah
More's poems were written, and when 'vital religion' began
its task in earnest. This need not be too much of a problem,
since the tendencies to such propaganda already existed.
But in any case there remain, of course, important
distinctions to be drawn between Blake's songs and those of
the Hannah More variety. Many of her poems describe a
small dramatic situation in which one protagonist is good,
the other bad. The situation is concrete and the ill-effects of
misbehaviour (drunkenness, for example, in 'Robert and
Richard'[13]) are vividly depicted. The narrator, who is
ostensibly objective, then draws a practical moral on the
basis of a common and intelligible event: drunkenness leads
to destitution.

But in Blake's 'The Chimney Sweeper' the narrator is
one of the sweeps, and the event from which the 'moral' is
drawn is a dream: it has no basis in the practical everyday
life of chimney sweeps. We have the option, then, of
regarding the dream as illusory comfort. One thing the
dream represents is the notion of ideology as a misunderstanding which favours dominant class economic interests.
Since we are permitting ourselves (with due caution) to
read later works by Blake we may also note that the 'Angel'
who tells Tom to 'be a good boy' (suspect phrase) is not
unlike the sanctimonious 'Angel' of *The Marrriage of Heaven
and Hell* who comes to 'Blake' and improvingly says, 'O
pitiable foolish young man! O horrible! O dreadful state!
consider the hot burning dungeon thou art preparing for

thyself to all eternity . . .' (pl. 17, E41/K155) This foolish young man was never a 'good boy'.

But the phrase 'be a good boy', like the moral, 'So if all do their duty, they need not fear harm', emphasizes that we are not merely speaking about the symbolic contents of a poem (a boy has a delusive dream). The particular words chosen are significant, and the words themselves can be attributed to indoctrination – but to indoctrination that has had its effect, that is now woven into the moral life and language of the child. Blake has a sense of the way artistic conventions and ordinary verbal usage are part of the operation of ideology. He sees that they weave (or bind) the texture of our mental life: submitting to 'mind-forg'd manacles' is not a matter of judiciously assenting to certain rational propositions, which may run counter to one's material interests, with more or less of a good grace. Neither is it a matter of pretending to accept alien notions 'imposed' by governing circles. 'Imposition' is more radical than that. For the manacles are made out of the conventions and words by which we live. Thus, although the chimney sweep finds comfort in a dream, the dream does have practical consequences:

> And so Tom awoke and we rose in the dark
> And got with our bags & our brushes to work.
> Tho' the morning was cold, Tom was happy & warm

The task of ideology is fulfilled: work discipline is maintained.

But, more than that, the dream appears to have made Tom 'happy and warm'. It has actually succeeded in mitigating the cruelty of his existence. The jaunty anapaestic metre underlines this fact. Indeed, from what we know of Blake's espousal of 'vision' it seems unlikely that we can simply dismiss the dream as 'false consciousness' in operation (to take one common meaning of 'ideology'). Without prejudice to the question, 'What is ideology?', it's clear that Blake didn't think it was only a system of illusory beliefs (though equally clearly that was *one* of the things he thought it was). He felt (to continue to translate his ideas into modern terms) that it was so much a mode of apprehending and surviving the social world that it could just as well be described as the general process of the production of meanings about society.

There is another element in the poem which is lacking from most of its precursor texts: pathos about children and the condition of the exploited. From Addison onwards the Pathetic had been seen as an aesthetic category contrasted with, and complementing, the Sublime. The former elicited tenderness and 'sentiment'; the latter was associated with 'grandeur' and elicited 'terror'. The ancestry of these ideas goes back to Aristotle and Longinus. But in the pre-Romantic period the fresh emphasis on the affective and emotional qualities of art gave them new primacy over mimetic and proportional criteria. Burke's *Enquiry into . . . the Sublime and Beautiful* (1756) disseminated a similar distinction very widely. Without an understanding of these ideas one misses much in the literature of the Romantic period. It would be possible, indeed, to claim that most of Wordsworth's poetry was written with one or both of these categories in mind: 'Two feelings have we also from the first, / [?] of grandeur and of tenderness.'[14] 'Grandeur' can be seen in the 'Crossing the Alps' section of *The Prelude*: 'tenderness' in such poems as 'The Idiot Boy' or 'Simon Lee'. Much of Wordsworth's poetry revolves around the question, 'How reconcile the awful, quasi-religious but optimistic promptings of the Sublime with the intolerable Pathos of human failure, loss and decline?'

'The head Sublime, the heart Pathos', says one of Blake's 'Proverbs of Hell' (*MHH*, pl. 10, E37/K152). And the distinction between Innocence and Experience, the Lamb and the Tyger, is congruent with this. Pathos, as the effect of a textual strategy designed to elicit pity, is lacking from the children's hymns and songs which influenced *Songs of Innocence*. This pathos, when taken together with the attitude to childhood in, say, 'Infant Joy', points to another characteristic Blake shares with a particular group of his contemporaries: the attempt at sympathetic identification

with children. Blake echoes several of Anna Letitia
Barbauld's *Hymns in Prose for Children* (1781) in *Songs of
Innocence*.[15] And Barbauld's 'Crew', as Lamb called them,
were very popular. In encouraging empathy with the child,
they catered for a taste which had also been fostered by
Rousseau, as Blake could also be said to do.[16] As with
Rousseau in *Emile*, so with writers such as Barbauld and
Mary Wollstonecraft, the child should not be subjected to
learning by rote, but educated through the pleasure it takes
in sensory experience and play. 'Education through the
senses' and sympathy for the child often end up, however,
in a cloyingly patronizing attitude. They can certainly seem
like more subtle means of indoctrination and control. And,
as Heather Glen remarks, the only associations Barbauld
seems to permit the child 'are those she herself points out'.
This is a passage from her third 'Hymn in Prose':

> But who is the shepherd's shepherd? who taketh care
> for him? who guideth him in the path he should go?
> and if he wander, who shall bring him back? God is
> the shepherd's shepherd. He is the Shepherd over all;
> he taketh care for all; the whole earth is his fold: we
> are all his flock; and every herb, and every green field,
> is the pasture which he hath prepared for us . . . God
> is our Shepherd, therefore we will follow him: God is
> our Father, therefore we will love him: God is our
> King, therefore we will obey him.[17]

Glen comments on this, 'One might well find Watts' honest
didacticism preferable to this ruthless insistence.'[18] But
insistence, if not relentlessness, is precisely the mark of
many of Blake's Songs of Innocence: 'The Lamb', 'Spring',
'A Cradle Song'. Or 'Infant Joy':

> I have no name
> I am but two days old. –
> What shall I call thee?
> I happy am
> Joy is my name, –
> Sweet joy befall thee!

Pretty joy!
Sweet joy but two days old,
Sweet joy I call thee;
Thou dost smile.
I sing the while
Sweet joy befall thee.

(E16/K118)

It is not insistence that differentiates Barbauld from Blake.
Rather, he shares her liberal attempt to enter into the
simple, supposedly repetitive speech of a child. Furthermore,
isn't 'Infant Joy' a striking instance of an adult putting
words into the mouth of a child? The first two lines can be
attributed to a child, though since it is only two days old we
may wonder, but the rest of the poem shows that they have
been imputed to it by another speaker – a speaker who
wishes to name the child, and to lend speech to its
inarticulacy: in each case fixing the indefinite with words:
possibly a suspect activity.

It is mere didacticism that separates Barbauld from
Blake, though of a less straightforward variety than that of
Watts. This indirect didacticism can be found in such
phrases as 'God is our Father, therefore we will love him:
God is our King, therefore we will obey him'. It is the
inference put into the child's mouth by the word 'therefore'
which reveals the subtle didacticism of Barbauld's hymn.
Nevertheless, one can imagine a child speaking these
words. It is possible that Blake learnt much from Barbauld:
the manner in which propaganda could indeed come out of
the mouths of babes once implanted in their minds; though
this is hardly the message Barbauld intended.

V

'The Chimney Sweeper' can be read, then, as a subtle
intervention in a debate about a pressing humanitarian
question. (Jonas Hanway's *A Sentimental History of Chimney
Sweeps*, published in 1785, had given a decisive push to the

movement to place constraints on the use of climbing boys, and this issued in a rather inadequate Parliamentary Bill.) Blake's intervention raises wider political issues of exploitation and indoctrination. Yet he refuses to treat indoctrination as 'imposition' in the sense of external compulsion. As in *The Marriage of Heaven and Hell*, so in 'The Chimney Sweeper', Blake rewrites the meaning of the word 'imposition': the little chimney sweep does not understand the Angelic trickery to which he is subject, and this limitation on his understanding is, in a sense, imposed by a discourse which is governed by alien class interests. And yet this limitation, with all that it distorts and obscures from view, gives shape and expression to the speaker's most cherished thoughts and affections.[19] Limitation is vehicle. Imposition is position. This fact is inscribed by Blake not in some radical moral fable (an inverted Watts) about the abuse of chimney sweeps, but in the words of a song which is both a parody and a poignant expression. Much of Blake's work foregrounds its own parodic nature in a way that avoids travesty. Blake was, often uneasily, aware of the dependence of discourse on conventions. To the extent that convention, by definition seemed incapable of conveying an absolutely present, original intention, Blake, who prized originality, was made anxious by it. But he also suspected that no intention whatsoever could be conveyed without it: hence the frequently ironic use of parody, or of forms which seems flawed or limited in some way.

One of the ways in which Blake signals the necessary limitation of *Innocence* is by means of the frame that surrounds many of the songs. We are now better placed to understand its function in the light of a concept of Derrida's, here described by Robert Young:

> The parergon, a word that Derrida finds in Kant, is the supplement to the 'ergon' (work) – against, beside, above and beyond it. In the visual arts, the parergon will be the frame, or drapery, or enclosing column. The parergon could also be a (critical) text, which

'encloses' another text. But what it precisely is not, is a simple inside/outside dichotomy.[20]

And Young goes on to quote Derrida:

Every analytic judgment presupposes that we can rigorously distinguish between the intrinsic and extrinsic. Aesthetic judgment *must* concern intrinsic beauty, and not the around and about. It is therefore necessary to know – this is the fundamental presupposition, the foundation – how to define the intrinsic, the framed, and what to exclude as frame *and* beyond the frame. We are thus *already* (i.e. although we are *at the margins*) at the unlocatable centre of the problem. Since, when we ask, 'What is a frame?', Kant responds, 'It is a parergon, a composite of inside and outside, but a composite which is not an amalgam or half-and-half, an outside which is called inside the inside to constitute it as inside.'[21]

Let us be clear: the frame is not the literal frame of a picture. The frame is the set of presuppositions, conventions and items of supposedly permitted knowledge about the work of art and its 'contents'. These things are not the work. But they constitute it. They are literally absent, but present in their effects. The point about the frame of a picture is that it is closely bound up with these facts: the frame is not the picture, but everything in the picture is composed in relation to it. It is therefore part of the composition of the picture, and is implicated in the aesthetic norms to which the picture adheres. Apparently outside the frame, the observer brings the supposedly external to bear on the picture. But this 'external' has already constituted the picture, and thus the observer is implicated in the action of the literal frame, as well as in what he or she brings to it.

Thus it would be absurd to claim that Blake's frames 'are' Derrida's 'parerga'. The parergon is an interpretative concept which could be applied to all works of art, and indeed to the very process by which something is deemed to be that strange thing, 'a work of art', at all. At the same time, paradoxically (and this is essential to the idea), the word reveals the limiting and fixing which occurs in all interpretation, and thus the impossibility of a final interpretation. For there is always more to be found in the work than a given interpretation can cope with, always something which might be deemed to contradict it. And thus the interpreter attempts to fix the unfixable: he 'frames' the work with partial evidence.

What is interesting about Blake's frames is that they can be seen as a metaphor for the paradoxical process described by Derrida. They are at the edges of the plates, but they are also integrated with the compositions: they shape themselves around the poems: leaves and tendrils grow into gaps in the shape of the text: this can be seen in both 'The Chimney Sweeper' and 'The Lamb' (figure 1). They are given the task of expressing the 'state' they frame, but at the same time they reveal the limitations of that state, and therefore the fact that there is much beyond the frame.

Working back from the graphic frames to the text, we can now see more clearly that Blake has 'framed' his innocents: he has depicted them as limited, and thus as requiring some other level of interpretation to explain them. But he has also exposed and, by implication, questioned his own framing of them: the graphic frames are an obtrusive fact about these designs – perhaps whoever put them there is actually doing some vicious limiting and fixing himself, as some of the adults in the songs do. This ironic manoeuvre can be seen in the most innocuous-seeming lyrics. The 'Introduction' sets the tone:

Piping down the valleys wild
Piping songs of pleasant glee
On a cloud I saw a child.
And he laughing said to me.

Pipe a song about a Lamb;
So I piped with merry chear,

Piper pipe that song again –
So I piped, he wept to hear.

Drop thy pipe thy happy pipe
Sing thy songs of happy chear,
So I sung the same again
While he wept with joy to hear

Piper sit thee down and write
In a book that all may read –
So he vanish'd from my sight.
And I pluck'd a hollow reed.

And I made a rural pen,
And I stain'd the water clear,
And I wrote my happy songs
Every child may joy to hear

(E7/K111)

The ways in which this poem acts as an introduction are obvious: a child, symbol of Innocence, directs the piping; the piper pipes a song about a 'Lamb', emblem of Innocence. Piping recalls the breath of inspiration. And the child, because 'On the cloud', not bound to the earth, is an even stronger symbol of freedom and spontaneity. It is as if some spiritual essence of innocence were directing itself into the form of pipe music. This is already a descent from the formless to the formed, though the form taken seems free and benign. But the piper is asked to write the songs down – at which point the source of inspiration vanishes. From one point of view the pen is as benign as the pipe: it is a 'hollow reed' and therefore, like the pipe, allows inspiration to pass through it. Yet we are alerted to the possibility that writing down the songs has corrupted the original inspiration by the idea of the staining of the clear water, as well as by the disappearance of the child, and, of course, the mere contrast of voice and writing. This hint of corruption could indicate that the state of Innocence is already fallen, already, to some extent, viciously formed, although at the same time containing much of value. According to this reading the 'rural pen' is another ambivalent notion, like 'state' itself: it is both expressive ('hollow reed') and limiting ('staining'). 'Naming' in 'Infant Joy', and writing in 'Introduction', are prime examples of Blake's ambivalence about form.

A hint of the unhappiness to be found in *Songs of Innocence* is provided by the weeping of the second stanza. True, it is preceded by 'laughing' and followed by weeping 'with joy'. But this pattern in itself suggests an artful mingling of two attitudes throughout the series of songs. It's easy to see that the chimney sweep has cause to weep (as he does: 'my father sold me while yet my tongue, / Could scarcely cry weep weep weep weep'). 'Laughing' occurs in Tom Dacre's dream, when the sweeps are all set free, and 'down a green plain leaping laughing they run'. It is important to remember the positive element in the songs: the parts of them that suggest the possibility of joyful and loving community. Another dream, in 'Night', expresses the old hope of the lion lying down with the lamb. Or perhaps vision is a better word: the poem envisages a flock guarded by angels who fend off 'wolves and tygers'. Sometimes the angels let one past them:

> When wolves and tygers howl for prey
> They pitying stand and weep;
> Seeking to drive their thirst away,
> And keep them from the sheep.
> But if they rush dreadful;
> The angels most heedful,
> Receive each mild spirit,
> New worlds to inherit.
>
> And there the lions ruddy eyes,
> Shall flow with tears of gold:
> And pitying the tender cries,
> And walking round the fold

(E14/K119)

But in the light of 'The Chimney Sweeper' it is possible to see the whole of 'Night' as another example of illusory comfort. Indeed, poems such as 'Night' and 'The Little Boy Found' can be seen as answering a need for security which is in itself potentially debilitating and enslaving. Innocence is a world where lost boys get found, where angels guard sheep, where God looks after little chimney sweeps. Such innocent imaginings are both witness to the possibility of loving community and severely limited misunderstandings of the world.

Yet it would be wrong to see 'laughing' and 'weeping' simply as two types of emotional expression to be found in Innocence. In *The Marriage of Heaven and Hell* there is a proverb, 'Excess of sorrow laughs. Excess of joy weeps' (E36/K151). Whatever else this may mean it certainly seems to imply a straining at the limits of contraries: when you take something far enough it verges on its opposite. Laughter and weeping in *Songs of Innocence* mark the bounds of the 'state' of Innocence: it is the form that laughter and weeping take, the extent to which the innocent speaker sees the necessity of laughing or weeping in any particular context, that defines the form of innocence. Thus, causes of weeping hint at the unknown world of *Experience*: in 'The Chimney Sweeper' they hint at the knowledge that children are brutally and cynically exploited. In 'The Blossom' they hint at the sexuality which is so little represented in 'Innocence':

Merry Merry Sparrow
Under leaves so green
A happy Blossom
Sees you swift as arrow
Seek your cradle narrow
Near my Bosom.

Pretty Pretty Robin
Under leaves so green
A happy Blossom
Hears you sobbing sobbing
Pretty Pretty Robin
Near my Bosom.   (E10/K115–16)

The blossom, the arrow, the 'cradle narrow', the bosom and the sobbing are clear pointers. But in *Innocence* weeping lacks the knowledge of *Experience*, as does the joy into which it turns so readily.

But the fact that a poem such as 'The Blossom' can appear in *Innocence* reminds us that the whole series of songs is a straining at the limits of the 'state' which supposedly defines them. There are constant hints of what lies beyond. But this is simply another way of saying that Blake's feelings about forms and 'states' are ambivalent.

VI

'The parergon could also be a (critical) text, which "encloses" another text', says Young.[22] We have seen the anxiety of critics to reduce the meaning of Blake's texts to something one-sided and uncontradictory. In the case of Hirsch this amounts to taking the ostensible frame of *Songs of Innocence* and ignoring the irony about framing which informs it. But we ourselves have offered a provisional interpretation of 'The Chimney Sweeper' in terms of the ideological conjuncture of the late eighteenth century, of its relation to the plight of chimney sweeps, and of Blake's understanding of what we now call 'ideology' not merely as 'false' consciousness, but as a means of comprehending and enduring social relations.

It might, however, be objected that such a view of 'The Chimney Sweeper' is reductionist and implies a reductionist interpretation of Blake. Isn't this another frame? After all, wasn't Blake a ghostic, a lover of alchemical symbolism, a neo-Platonist? Of 'The Chimney Sweeper' Kathleen Raine remarks that 'The "soot" is the earthly mire and clay that cannot defile the spirit' and quotes a passage from Plotinus to support this view. She goes on to cite Thomas Taylor's *Dissertation on the Mysteries*, where he recalls Empedocles:

Lamenting his connection with this corporeal world he pathetically exclaims:

> *For this I weep, for this indulge my woe*
> *That e'er my soul such novel realms should know.*

Plato, too, it is well known, considered the body as the sepulchre of the soul; and in the *Cratylus* consents with the doctrine of Orpheus, that the soul is punished through its union with body . . . The Pythagorean Philolaus [writes] 'that the soul is united with body for the sake of suffering punishment, and that it is buried in the body as in a sepulchre'.[23]

'Weep' and 'woe' in the couplet, as well as the idea of being shut in a coffin ('sepulchre') might seem to support the case that Blake was thinking of this passage when he wrote 'The Chimney Sweeper'. Nevertheless, one might not find the case conclusive. But Raine goes on to cite a passage from another arcane writer whose works were undoubtedly known to Blake: Swedenborg. In *Concerning the Earths in our Solar System* Swedenborg writes of certain inhabitants of Jupiter:

There are also Spirits amongst those from the Earth Jupiter, whom they call Sweepers of Chimneys, because they appear in like Garments, and likewise with sooty faces . . . One of these spirits came to me, and anxiously requested that I would intercede for him to be admitted into heaven . . . at that Instant the Angel called to him to cast off his Raiment, which he did immediately with inconceivable Quickness from the Vehemence of his Desire . . . I was informed that such, when they are prepared for Heaven, are stripped of their own Garments, and are cloathed with new shining Raiment, and become Angels.[24]

Since Blake had read Swedenborg, this passage is very likely to have been a source for the poem. Further, it lends greater credence to the claims of Plotinus and Thomas Taylor. But the issue cannot be proven one way or the other. Such cases can help to answer an important question, but they cannot clinch it: Was Blake substantially influenced by arcane traditions such as those Raine refers to? Did he, indeed, in a sense *belong* to those traditions? If he did, then whatever the claims of any particular source (so often unprovable and sometimes uninteresting) we may be missing much in Blake unless we read him in the light of the Hermetic tradition (the tradition of seeing spiritual significance in alchemy) and of neo-Platonism, Kabbalism and other occult doctrines.

Such an idea has been anathema to some critics, often Marxists, because it seems to detract from the idea of Blake as a social critic. Can we retain our provisional model of Blake as a radical poet, albeit one possessed of 'romantic irony'? For chimney sweeps as exploited victims might seem quite different from chimney sweeps as arcane emblems of our corporeal clay. Paul Fauvet has these hostile words to say about the occultists:

> Others, confronted with Blake's presentation of eighteenth century realities, sidestep them within lengthy ramblings about Blake's alleged borrowings from Swedenborg and neo-platonism. The prime sinner here is Kathleen Raine, who appears to believe that poetry is vastly improved if its content is ignored while the critic ransacks the most unlikely and obscure corners for 'source material'. Do we really need to have heard of, let alone read, Everard's translation of the *Hermetics* (*The Divine Pymander*) or Thomas Taylor's *Dissertation on the Mysteries* to understnad [sic] *The Chimney Sweeper* . . .?[23]

For Fauvet it is as plain as day that 'The Chimney Sweeper' simply reveals the plight of chimney sweeps, and in so doing questions the 'dominant' ideology in the light of 'reality'.

The trouble with Kathleen Raine is that her readings suggest that Blake *was* on the side of the angels. But we should not be tempted, in opposition to her, by what seems to modern readers a more digestible account: tempted, that is, to take it for granted, like Fauvet, that Blake was some kind of incipient historical materialist who scorned the occult. Fauvet never asks about the specific nature of Blake's literary production. The kinds of sources he mentions are illuminating, but there's nothing particularly new about them. What is worrying is the tendency for Marxist criticism to degenerate into a 'study of *similarities* between Blake and Marx', as David Punter says.[26] With reference to Fauvet's article: what, for instance, is the 'dominant ideology', associated with the ruling 'class', and what is the 'reality' in terms of which it is unmasked?[27] What are Blake's means of access to this 'reality'? The fact is that there was no unified, dominant ideology: 'Deism', or 'Natural Religion' (rational religion), took radical and conservative forms; conservatives might or might not be in a broad sense 'Deistical'; Blake was *always* savagely anti-Deist in principle, but found common political cause with radical Deists such as Paine. A complex situation.

And Blake is complex. For there is really no point in ignoring the arcane connections of much of his writing. What is gained by doing so? For Fauvet, to admit that Blake had eagerly devoured many vast tomes of obscure alchemical and neo-Platonic writings (as he undoubtedly had) would be to call his perception of 'reality' into question. Blake must be a Marxist *avant la lettre*. That is how he is able to perceive 'reality'. But the aim of Marxist criticism is not to find friends among the great writers, even though it may end up by doing so. It is to explain the genesis of texts in class society as described by historical materialism. It may also be to suggest how writers may make effective political interventions in society. Further, it may seek to inquire whether these two apparently separate aims are related. But it should not feel threatened by the idea that Blake was interested in alchemy, any more than by the fact that John Donne was an Anglican.

Blake placed himself firmly in the tradition of philosophical alchemy: he claimed six great influences on himself:

Now my lot in the Heavens is this, Milton lov'd me
    in childhood & shew'd me his face.
Ezra came with Isaiah the Prophet, but Shakespeare
    in riper years gave me his hand;
Paracelsus & Behmen appear'd to me terrors appear'd
    in the Heavens above
And in Hell beneath . . .
            (Letter to Flaxman, 12 Sept. 1800, K799)

Paracelsus and 'Behmen' (Boehme) were philosophical alchemists: they were interested in the spiritual meaning that can be attached to alchemical symbols. Blake's relationship with their tradition was critical and cavalier. Characteristically he often inverts its values. Indeed, Fauvet himself is very near the mark when he mentions, *à propos* of 'The Chimney Sweeper', Joseph Wicksteed's assertion that 'an earthy darkness of the flesh is escaped spiritually'! Fauvet adds, 'the difference is that Wicksteed approves of this, and Blake doesn't'.[28] Quite: Blake uses the complex and ramified symbolism of a tradition marked by dualism of mind and body in order to attack that dualism: such ideas are instilled by 'Angels'.

Fauvet is asking a difficult question when he demands to know if we need to have read the *Hermetics* of Thomas Taylor in order to understand 'The Chimney Sweeper'. Readers do not *need* to read anything: they have always already read something and thus will arrive at some sort of understanding. But, if the question is whether Blake's work as a whole makes reference to the occult tradition, the answer must surely be that it does. Only by some very purist notion of the text can one ignore the hermeticist and neo-Platonic connections evoked by the prophetic books. In the context of Blake's work as a whole Raine's claim that the sweep's soot 'is the earthly mire and clay that cannot defile the spirit' is certainly not as far-fetched as some people would like to think.

But Blake inverts the values of the occult tradition. He believes that body and Soul are one. God and the Angel in

'The Chimney Sweeper' have imposed the conditions in which Tom Dacre has to live. God and the Angel are responsible for the dream of being washed white and free of soot. God and the Angel represent and impose the idea of a separation between body and spirit. And, in so far as Blake may be alluding to Swedenborg's use of sooty garments as a metaphor for the earthly clay, it is partly to impugn the cruelty and false hopes which such metaphors can sustain. In 'The Everlasting Gospel' (*c.*1818 : note the late date – some of Blake's opinions didn't change much) he says of himself and of an enemy with opposed ideas. 'Both read the Bible day & night, / But though read'st black where I read white': black for the literal sense (the letters), white for the meaning. Kathleen Raine has read the Bible, and she has useful things to say about Blake's reading of it. But too often she reads black where he reads white. And she tends to do the same with neo-Platonism.

But we have still not quite done with 'The Chimney Sweeper'. To return to our reading: according to this the tainted vehicle of children's hymns and religious platitudes carries all the spontaneous longings of the speaker and of Tom Dacre – therein lies the poignancy of the poem. By the same token the idea of being released from black coffins and washed of soot is not merely Blake's knowing exposure of Angels' hypocritical promises and dualist mentality. It is that, certainly. But because it comes to us on the lips of an unknowing and unhappy sweep it also testifies to the humanity sweeps share with the reader, carrying, as it does, the idea of a happy communal state.

So complex are these apparently simple songs. Their complexity is only matched by the multitidue of differing and reductionist readings they evoke from critics.

VII

But where does our acceptance of the occultist side of Blake leave our picture of him as a radical? Perhaps it is time to advance a hypothesis concerning Blake's true precursors, and his ideological position.

E.P. Thompson says, near the beginning of *The Making of the English Working class*, that '*Pilgrim's Progress* is, with *Rights of Man*, one of the two foundation texts of the English working-class movement.'[29] It would also be true to say that these two books together can conveniently stand for a major contradiction in Blake's work, which does lie at this confluence of politically radical rationalism and politically radical Protestantism. Nevertheless, it is not accurate to say, as Thompson does, that Blake felt himself 'torn between a rational Deism' (the idea of rational religion which tended to be held by radicals) and the spiritual beliefs of the sects. Rather, he accepted only the political prescriptions of the rationalists and their allies, while rejecting the terms upon which these prescriptions were based, in favour of more venerable, radical Christian ideas. Such a position hardly permits access to 'reality', if by that is meant the access permitted by an understanding of Marxism. We may find Blake sympathetic, but his writings are as *deformative* of reality as any imaginative works must be. At the same time we may feel that they do convey a complete understanding of the forces at work in this period than those of some others.

Blake's Liberty is not the individualistic, bourgeois conception of his poetic contemporaries. His allegiance is to Bunyan ('Protestantism') rather than to Tom Paine (libertarian rationalism). Or, more accurately, it is to the 'underground' tradition of antinomian, or libertarian, radical Protestantism which survived from the Civil War period right down to the end of the eighteenth century. It is some time now since A.L. Morton documented the similarity of some of Blake's terms and concepts with those of the Ranters.[30] The survival of the Mugletonians, and the 'prophecies' of contemporaries of Blake, such as Richard Brothers and Joanna Southcott, support the view that radical Protestantism may still have been influential outside the 'polite' world in the late eighteenth century. It is therefore intriguing to note that an interest in Paracelsus and Boehme was very common among the sects of the English Revolution period.[31] The radical Blake and the arcane Blake probably belong to the same tradition, a fact which renders futile the urge of critics to pick one and play down the other. It is because this tradition only produced one major artist that Blake used to seem so absolutely *sui generis*.

This model of Blake can be made more subtle: his occupation as commercial engraver moves him towards the middle class. He comes into contact with fashionable literary theories, styles and movements. Hence his use of the Sublime and his imitations of the fashionable *Ossian*. Blake's Milton is not only the Protestant prophet of Christian Liberty, but also the most favoured candidate for 'sublimity' in the modish cult of the Sublime. Blake, then, combines both old artisanal and new middle-class political and artistic ideologies: Bunyan meets both Paine and Romantic sensibility and sublimity. This is a useful way of understanding Blake. But there are two important qualifications to be made. First, it only provides the conditions of existence of Blake's work: relatively empty categories, essential to explanation and description, but tending to reductionism unless filled out by more minute formal description which allows for the autonomy of artistic tradition. Secondly, the strange meeting of Enlightenment rationalism, antinomian Protestantism and Romantic sensibility cannot be conceived as a crude aggregate in which these ideologies are simply added onto each other. There are elements in each tradition which conflict with elements in the others. Blake had to solve these contradictions, or find a quasi-solution. For Bunyan and Paine don't mix. Bunyan, Paine, Boehme and Rousseau make an even stranger combination. This book will go on to claim that such a curious conjuncture means that Blake has to 'graft' different discourses onto each other, to borrow a term from Derrida. But, when ideas from different traditions are spliced together, naturally 'their sense and their function change', as Derrida says.[32] As for *Songs of Innocence*, we have already seen that 'The Chimney Sweeper' is the product of grafts: children's hymns, liberal educational theories and occult emblems. Furthermore, for what the term is worth, it is highly self-conscious in its grafting: it exposes the graft. We shall claim that there are historical reasons why Blake's grafting was so self-conscious. And we shall also claim that his work is marked by deep anxiety about whether the discourses and conventions he uses are tainted parasites, grafted onto some original tree of meaning, or whether it is impossible to articulate any idea in the 'Fallen World', as Blake called it, without it being tainted. The chimney sweeper's position is similar to Blake's in that both employ tainted conventions.

2 *Songs of Experience*

Although readers still come to *Songs of Innocence* with preconceptions that rule out irony, they generally change their minds in the end. Among critics the idea that there is an ironic element commands almost universal assent. In *Experience*, by contrast, preconception and subsequent readings seem to agree: 'Experience' is an unfortunate (but possibly necessary) state; the speakers of the poems, in so far as they angrily perceive the ills of society, are meant to be justified. This consensus still leaves a few loose ends for critics to worry over: Just how 'bad' is Experience, seeing that it is inevitable? In what sense is it necessary? These questions are bound up with the interpretation of problem poems such as 'The Tyger': is the Tyger good, bad, or ambivalent?[1] In fact there are good grounds for thinking that the Songs of Experience are indeed, like the Songs of Innocence, marked by irony, especially about the represented speakers. If this is true then even the righteous wrath of the speaker of 'London' is subject to implied criticism – though this is not the same thing as saying that it is only criticism that is implied.

An obvious difference between *Innocence* and *Experience* lies in the critical and disillusioned attitude of the speakers in the latter, and in the way this affects the very texture of the verse. This difference makes it seem easier, at first glance, to judge the tone of the *Experience* speaker. One may well worry about how to interpret lines from *Innocence* such as 'So if all do their duty they need not fear harm' or 'Then cherish pity lest you drive an angel from your door'. But surely there can be no doubt about this:

> Because I was happy upon the heath,
> And smil'd among the winters snow:
> They clothed me in the clothes of death,
> And taught me to sing the notes of woe.
>
> ('The Chimney Sweeper')

Or this:

> In every cry of every Man,
> In every Infants cry of fear,
> In every voice: in every ban,
> The mind-forg'd manacles I hear
>
> ('London')

The clearest way for the reader to interpret *Songs of Experience* is as an unveiling of the horrors hidden from the eye of Innocence. The system of parallels, where an *Experience* song has the same title as an *Innocence* one with which it is contrasted, makes this a natural reading.

The verse itself enforces the contrast. In *Innocence* the language is seldom figurative. Statements are generally submitted to the dictates of a brief narrative. To take some lines almost at random:

> My mother taught me underneath a tree
> And sitting down before the heat of day,
> She took me on her lap and kissed me
>
> ('The Little Black Boy')

> Old John with white hair
> Does laugh away care,
> Sitting under the oak,
> Among the old folk.
> They laugh at our play,
> And soon they all say,
> Such such were the joys.
> When we all girls & boys,

In our youth time were seen,
On the Ecchoing Green.

('The Ecchoing Green')

Of course, the strategy of many Songs of Innocence is to
nudge the reader into a perception that these simple
narratives take their place in a subtle ironic allegory. In
which case their unelaborated figures take on greater
figurativeness. But the language itself is not usually highly
figured. When it is it operates to represent the innocent
speaker as ingenuously impressed by appearances, unable
to pass beyond them – though investing them with beauty:

O what a multitude they seemd these flowers of
London town
Seated in companies they sit with radiance all their
own
The hum of multitudes was there but multitides of
lambs
Thousands of little boys & girls raising their innocent
hands

Now like a mighty wind they raise to heaven the voice
of song
Or like harmonious thunderings the seats of heaven
among

('Holy Thursday')

Here metaphor and simile abound. Again, 'multitudes of
lambs' takes its place in an ironic allegory: the lamb is a
sacrificial victim. But this irony cannot be attributed to the
speaker, for whom the image is descriptive. And 'flowers',
'mighty wind' and 'harmonious thunderings' are descriptive
figures: they give an impression. Thus they take their place
with the even more ingenuous line earlier in the poem: 'The
children walking two & two in red & blue & green'.

By contrast the language of *Experience* could sometimes be
described as 'conceited':

But most thro' midnight streets I hear
How the youthful Harlots curse

Blasts the new-born Infants tear
And blights with plagues the Marriage hearse
                                        ('London')

The paradox 'Marriage hearse' is knowing, disillusioned, conceptual. The whole stanza, though it contains a powerful descriptive moment, is basically a general statement expressed in a striking compound metaphor in the last three lines. To paraphrase: 'The youthful harlot's curse may be venereal disease, in which case it causes the eyes of her congenitally afflicted child to run. It also infects the marriage bed. But there is poetic justice in this, for marriage and prostitution are mutually dependent institutions. In any case, marriage is already a living death.' There is more to be said about these lines, and about 'London'. But we have said enough to establish that the contrast between Innocence and Experience should not be conceived merely as a contrast between two attitudes. For it is also a related contrast in the use of poetic language. Where the language is not as 'conceited' as that of 'London', the poem may clearly signal its allegorical nature:

I went to the Garden of Love.
And saw what I never had seen:
A Chapel was build in the midst,
Where I used to play on the green.

And the gates of this Chapel were shut,
And Thou shalt not. writ over the door
                                    ('The Garden of Love')

Or else it may simply make an abstract, general comment:

Pity would be no more,
If we did not make somebody Poor:
And Mercy no more could be,
If all were as happy as we
                                    ('The Human Abstract')

But in all these cases we may impute a demystifying

knowledge to the represented speaker: this knowledge reveals the exploitation and repression practiced by society's rulers (the 'Priest & King') which they cloak in 'Mystery' (see 'The Human Abstract'). Thus the movement from Innocence to Experience certainly conforms in a general way to the idea of a movement from ignorance to knowledge.

But if Innocence and Experience are the 'Two Contrary States of the Human Soul', and if 'Without Contraries is no progression', does the soul constantly oscillate between joyous ignorance and joyless knowledge? That would be too crude a summary. For the joy is as important as the knowledge, and, indeed, constitutes a form of knowledge for Blake. The frame of Innocence is also a barrier: the eye of Innocence stops at appearances, as in 'Holy Thursday'. But the appearances are transformed by imagination: the barrier is decorated with leaves. It may be quite as bad, or worse, to be surrounded by a leafless frame. For, while the stripping of the leaves corresponds to the rending of the veils of Mystery, a barrier still remains – and one that is unadorned by imagination.

II

'London' is a poem which strikingly illustrates Blake's ambivalence about the demystifying savagery of the speakers of Experience:

> I wander thro' each charter'd street,
> Near where the charter'd Thames does flow.
> And mark in every face I meet
> Marks of weakness, marks of woe.
>
> In every cry of every Man,
> In every Infants cry of fear,
> In every voice: in every ban,
> The mind-forg'd manacles I hear

How the Chimney-sweepers cry
Every blackning Church appalls,
And the hapless Soldiers sigh
Runs in blood down Palace walls

But most thro' midnight streets I hear
How the youthful Harlots curse
Blasts the new-born Infants tear
And blights with plagues the Marriage hearse
(E26–7/K216)

Perception which transcends appearance is a theme of each stanza. In the first the speaker sees 'marks of woe' in the faces of passers-by; in the second he hears the 'mind-forg'd manacles' of ideology in the voices and cries of a London street; in the third he is able to perceive the guilt for the sufferings of chimney sweeps and soldiers being ascribed to its true bearers, Church and Palace (Priest and King again). In the fourth the sound of the harlot's curse drives him to thoughts of the mutual dependence of marriage and prostitution.

But the speaker could be seen as investing his surroundings with a partial interpretation. Many commentators have marked the insistent repetition of the word 'mark' in the first stanza, and the fact that the verb 'to mark' (l. 3) can mean both 'to notice' and 'to inscribe upon': the speaker could be thought of as inscribing marks of weakness and woe on those whom he encounters. The third stanza, I should add, repeats the notion of marking: the metaphorical blood that runs down the palace walls is a mark unseen by any other. The chimney sweep's cry changes the colour of the churches (makes them pale). The poem alternates between sight and sound: stanzas 1 and 3 refer to visual marking; stanzas 2 and 4 to hearing, to auditory marking. This patterning emphasizes the inclusiveness of the speaker's interpretation: it comprehensively covers both sight and sound. The very insistence of the phrase 'In every . . .' suggests inclusiveness: there are no exceptions here. This overwhelming and oppressive all-inclusiveness of horror implies that the speaker is to some extent trapped within his own interpretation.

This sense of entrapment is no more devoid of a social meaning, however, than are the more obvious references of the poem. Walter Benjamin writes that 'Fear, revulsion, and horror were the emotions which the big-city crowd aroused in those who first observed it.'[2] By the time Blake wrote of it London was already a big city in Benjamin's sense. It would be quite wrong to equate Blake's wandering speaker with Benjamin's description of Baudelaire's *flâneur* ('stroller', 'idler'), who is a 'man of leisure' and is 'unwilling to forgo the life of a gentleman of leisure'.[3] Nevertheless, Blake's speaker is isolated in the city crowd, and experiences something akin to what Engels describes in a passage from *The Condition of the Working Class in England* which Benjamin cites:

> Only when one has tramped the pavements of the main streets for a few days does one notice that these Londoners have had to sacrifice what is best in human nature in order to create all the wonders of civilization with which their city teems, that a hundred creative faculties that lay dormant in them remained inactive and were suppressed . . . There is something distasteful about the very bustle of the streets, something that is abhorrent to human nature itself[4]

Blake's poem describes the first appearance of the 'amorphous mass', as Benjamin calls it, which Marx realized should be 'forged into the iron of the proletariat'.[5] Although Benjamin refers to a later period of capitalism, Blake and his contemporaries were already aware of 'alienation'. 'London' does not describe the crowd itself in terms that suggest alienation. But the isolated speaker's wandering through the crowd is alienated and sets the whole poem in the context of alienation. Like Poe and Baudelaire, Blake actively interprets the equivocal and amorphous mass, 'marking' it. But this marking is itself questioned: it is typical of Blake that his poems readily permit an ironic reading in which the speaker is himself damagingly marked by alienation. Nor is this a trivial irony: on the contrary, it is one more instance of Blake's serious irony: in none of his works is he able to comfort the reader with a discourse which can be safely fixed as authoritative 'meta-commentary'.[6] Indeed, the attempt to find such a secure vantage point was recognized by Blake as sterile and authoritarian. It is Urizen who 'abstracts' in this way: 'But unknown, abstracted / Brooding secret, the dark power hid' (*Book of Urizen*, 3:6–7).

> From the depths of dark solitude. From
> The eternal abode in my holiness,
> Hidden set apart in my stern counsels
> Reserv'd for the days of futurity,
> I have sought for a joy without pain,
> For a solid without fluctuation
>
> (4:6–11, E71/K224)

An important irony of *The Book of Urizen* is that even this sterile retreat is in fact dependent for its continuation on the activities of Los, the Poetic Genius, who thus becomes responsible not only for the creation of 'Living Form', but also for that of dead form. Urizen forms 'a dividing rule', 'scales to weigh' and 'golden compasses' (20:25–39). He thus measures what has really been created by the prolific Los. He imagines that in doing so he himself is creating, whereas in fact he is abstracting from ('devouring') the creations of Los.[7] We shall see that *Experience* is a state equivalent, not to Urizen's world as he perceives it, but to Los's being implicated in the creation of limited and oppressive form: this becomes evident when one considers the role of the Bard in the 'Introduction' to *Experience*, as we shall do in the next chapter. It is for this reason that, even where, as in 'London', the speaker is signalled as 'sympathetic', we are forced to conclude that his perspective is severely limited. But this is a bitter, as well as a subtle, irony, which derives from Blake's acute awareness of the political consequences of not being able to establish a point of pure perception outside the ideologies, discourses and, indeed, struggles of his own time. The bitterness is very close to that expressed by Brecht in 'To Posterity':

> And yet we know well:
> Even hatred of vileness
> Distorts a man's features.
> Even anger at injustice
> Makes hoarse his voice. Ah, we
> Who desired to prepare the soil for kindness
> Could not ourselves be kind.
>
> (T. Michael Hamburger)

The irony derives from the fact that Blake was less optimistic than Brecht about his paradox. For, while he definitely could not doubt the necessity of anger at injustice, neither could he trust that love would ever come of anger. So that many Songs of Experience give the impression of a harsh grating indignation, unrelieved by any sense of possible development. And we know that Blake thought that such a sense was necessary. The leafless frame, denuded of deceptive foliage, is truly perceived as a limit. The Songs of Experience celebrate Energy, Wrath: they thus align themselves with the voice of the 'Prolific'. But the speakers are prolifics who are not only being devoured, but also know that they are being devoured. The 'Devourer' corresponds to the limited perspective imposed by Priest and King: it is the frame, whether in *Innocence* or *Experience*. But in *Experience*, unlike *Innocence*, it is perceived as a limit: as the 'outward bound or circumference of Energy' (*MHH*, pl. 4).

III

What we have been saying about 'London' may seem to leave the poem stranded between two readings: one which see it as a critique of a social system; and another which sees it as ironic about the speaker. The possibility of seeing irony in the poem has long been recognized. Indeed, Jonathan Culler makes it an exemplar of the 'openness' of literary works. What he says is worth quoting at length:

> it is important to stress that if we want to understand the nature of literature and of our adventures in language we will have to recognize that the 'openness' and 'ambiguity' of literary works result not from vagueness nor from each reader's desire to project himself into the work, but from the potential reversibility of every figure. Any figure can be read referentially or rhetorically. 'My love is a red, red rose' tells us, referentially, of desirable qualities that the beloved possesses. Read rhetorically, in its figurality, it indicates a desire to see her as she is not: as a rose. 'Charter'd street' in the first stanza of 'London' tells us, referentially, of an ordered city its streets full of chartered institutions. Rhetorically, it is hyperbole: to speak as if even the streets had royal charters is excessive, ironic. One can, of course, go on to read this irony referentially, as a suggestion that too many charters enslave: London is so restrictive that even streets need charters to exist. But one could also in turn reverse this figure and, reading the irony in its figurality, say that the act of seeing streets as if they were chartered is an example of another kind of enslavement: enslavement to one's own fiction. These four readings are generated by two elementary operations which, as a pair, constitute the possibility of figural reading.[8]

It's interesting that Blake should generate such readings – or such consciousness of reading. For, though Culler's four readings can indeed be applied to all literary works, it is often easier for the reader to treat one of these readings as more appropriate than the others. Indeed, readers tend too eagerly to accept signals in the text that such and such a reading is appropriate. They will then refer to this reading as representing the author's 'intention', and thus as authoritative. It is very difficult to establish such signals with Blake. And, indeed, not only 'openness', but the particular kind of openness analysed here, is typical of him. For irony combined with the 'irony of irony' (the ironic speaker is himself limited) is characteristic of all Blake's work.

Culler goes on to assert that 'The opposing, even contradictory, readings engendered in this way depend not on prior "opinions" of the subject but on formal operations that constitute the activity of interpretation.'[9] But this distinction between 'opinions' and 'formal operations' is ill-grounded. For 'opinions' imply 'formal operations': if you have certain opinions, you will tend to engage in certain formal operations linked to those opinions. On the other hand, 'formal operations' are not picked at random by neutral, value-free, opinionless readers: readers will engage in such and such operations rather than others because these operations fit with their world view. This world view will not be a matter of free-floating, capricious 'opinions'. It will be marked by a structure of beliefs which will imply a whole range of practices, including that of 'reading literature'. This structure of beliefs has to be described in political terms. Literary criticism cannot solve these problems in a vacuum. There is no reason within the terms of so-called literary criticism why one should prefer one type of reading over another. The reasons why people do so are political.

Since this is so it is hardly surprising that Marxist and other radical critics have tended to see such a poem as Blake's 'London' as a critique of a social system (Culler's 'referential' readings) while professional critics with an interest in literary theory tend to see it as ironic about the speaker (Culler's 'rhetorical' readings).

But the truth is that this is a sterile conflict. For all linguistic acts can be seen as referential, since they can all be ascribed a context. But they can all also be seen as rhetorical, and this is as true of 'philosophical' texts and of conversations on the bus as it is of 'literary' texts.[10]

Metaphor, poetic interpretation, lurks in the most neutral-seeming language.

This means that we are all properly the object of the same irony that applies to the speaker in 'London'. Even at our most accurate and 'scientific' we are to some extent trapped within the limits of our historically relative position. A Marxist criticism which is aware of the implication of human subjects in signifying practices which ensure the impossibility of access to abstract Truth, and which make nonsense of the idea of univocal intention, is well placed to conduct properly sensitive analyses of the relations between the 'referential' and the 'rhetorical' in such a poem as 'London'. The price of this advance, however, will have to be the recognition that the 'referential' only ever appears in rhetorical form.

'History', which some critics make the extra-literary arbiter of literary reference, is itself only present to us in the various rhetorics which make up dusty records and 'current affairs' as much as they do the works of Gibbon or Macaulay. This is not an abnegation of the task of understanding history. Rather it is a statement of the challenge involved in doing so. 'Il n'y a pas de hors texte', says Derrida. But he also says that 'The legitimate renunciation of a certain style of causality perhaps does not give one the right to renounce all etiological demands.'[11] I take it that he is talking about the facile recourse to History, and a concomitant tendency to treat literary texts as simple expressions of a tradition conceived in linear and non-contradictory terms; and that he means that, though one must reject this facility, one cannot say that there are no such things as causes or influences or traditions.

The perspective outlined above might not seem very orthodox to some Marxists. Yet Marx himself was always aware of the historically relative position of even the most enlightened observer. As he says in his third thesis on Feuerbach;

The [mechanical] materialist doctrine concerning the

changing of circumstances and education forgets that circumstances are changed by men and that the educator must himself be educated. This doctrine has therefore to divide society into two parts, one of which is superior to society.[12]

Hardly Derridean. But consistent with the perspective we have outlined. For Marx, then, even the revolutionary must, in the nature of things, be implicated in reactionary ideologies. He or she cannot stand outside them.

Blake, on the other hand, puts poignancy into the second-hand phrases of the chimney sweep while at the same time revealing the limitations of the righteously indignant speaker of 'London'. Speakers are trapped within the limitations of interpretation, but they also find value within them. And they do refer to 'History'.

Once one has lodged the important *caveat* against rushing to History and the 'referential', one is free to return to them, chastened and with caution. Rejecting the idea of an immediately accessible referent outside somebody's interpretation, one may still construct a sense of the history of which a literary work is part, though this may be a difficult and uncertain process. William Ray expresses the hope that 'future critics will recover, on the far side of irony's absolute freedom, the charm of simple historical (arti)fact'.[13] Where else is there to go?

'London' resounds with the echoes of its historical context. The word 'charter'd' in the first stanza, for instance. In the early 'King Edward the Third' Blake himself had referred to 'Liberty, the charter'd right of Englishmen'. And, as E.P. Thompson points out, there are 'endless examples' in the eighteenth century of references to 'chartered rights, chartered liberties, magna carta: the word is at the centre of Whig ideology'.[14] But Blake had doubts about 'chartered liberty' on two scores: first, he simply doubted that liberty had in fact been granted to most English people; secondly, as Thompson well says, 'A charter of liberty is, simultaneously, a denial of these liberties to others.'[15] And he quotes Tom Paine, who puts the matter sucinctly in *Rights of Man*:

> Every chartered town is an aristocratical monopoly in itself, and the qualification of electors proceeds out of those chartered monopolies. Is this freedom?

> It is a perversion to say that a charter gives rights. It operates by a contrary effect – that of taking rights away. Rights are inherently in all the inhabitants; but charters, by annulling those rights in the majority, leave the right, by exclusion, in the hands of a few . . .[16]

Blake's poem thus inserts itself into 'the biggest political argument that was agitating Britain in 1791–3'.[17] But quite as interesting for our discussion is the fact that 'charter'd' is another of those ambiguous Blakean words that expresses freedom and limitation simultaneously: in an obvious sense, freedom for some and the lack of it for others; in a more subtle sense, a limited form of freedom even for the lucky few. Its use is precisely analogous to that of the word 'imposition' in *The Marriage*. But unlike 'imposition' it's a word that evokes the idea of writing or inscription. The word 'charter'd' and the word 'mark' in the same stanza are mutually enriching.

IV

There is an interesting critical debate about how far the word 'mark' alludes to uses of the word in the Bible. This debate reflects on the way we regard the represented speaker. Harold Bloom, among others, suggests that the word refers to Ezekiel 9:4:

> And the Lord said unto him, 'Go through the midst of the city, through the midst of Jerusalem, and set a mark upon the foreheads of the men that sigh and that cry for all the abominations that be done in the midst thereof.'

And to the others he said in mine hearing, 'Go ye after him through the city, and smite: let not your eyes spare, neither have ye pity:

'Slay utterly old and young, both maids, and little children, and women: but come not near any man upon whom is the mark . . .'

Bloom claims that this is the 'precursor-text' of Blake's 'London'. If so, the obvious interpretation of the poem would be: the suffering people are righteous, the Church and King damned. But Bloom rejects this as a 'weak, unproductive' misreading.[18] Rather, according to him, Ezekiel is present as the precise measure by which Blake reveals that he himself is also 'weak and woeful, and not the Ezekiel-like prophet he should be', and that he has repressed this knowledge.[19] And indeed this highly original reading does reinforce our sense of the speaker's being implicated in the evil he perceives. It also helps to explain how the prophet who would seem to 'mark' (inscribe) is really the weak, woeful and alienated observer who marks in the sense of merely noticing, and is himself marked by not being Ezekiel.

Bloom notes that 'charter'd' and 'mark' both contain the idea of *writing*.[20] The 'marker' in Ezekiel is a 'writer'. Writing in 'London' is contrasted to the 'lost prophetic *voice*' for which Blake feels a 'terrifying nostalgia'. For Bloom this means the poem is profoundly 'anti-Derridaean'.[21] For Derrida is a critic of the idea that the voice represents the truest, because most spontaneous and 'present', expression. But it should be said that Derrida believes this idea to be inescapable in Western culture. We have already noted the typically Blakean notion of the sign containing the possibility both of freedom and of limitation. It seems to me that the accent here is on limitation. 'Devoured' by the outlines or boundaries set by others' freedom ('charter'd'), the poet is unable freely to set a 'mark' but can only passively observe. In this way the poem accords with what we have said about the state of

Experience in general. Indeed, it's crucial for constructing our sense of what Experience is.

But we must return to Bloom's rejection of the idea that Blake is separating sheep and goats, people and rulers, in the way that Ezekiel does. For in making a 'strong misreading' Bloom, like other critics, rushes to exclude what seems unruly or inconsistent. Why shouldn't Blake think the people would be saved and the rulers damned? He was a radical, after all. Of course, this reading is inconsistent with the one that stated that we're all marked for damnation, people and rulers alike. But we've already rejected the idea that poems must be shown to be internally consistent. The ironic thing is that Bloom's 'strong misreading' actually presupposes some reference to the idea of separating people and rulers. For if Blake really was nostalgic for the voice of the prophet he would also have been nostalgic for the prophet's role – which was to express the righteous indignation of God, and foretell the punishment of the wicked, in this case the Church and King. So, even if Blake doesn't feel up to that, that is what he doesn't feel up to.

But, if we make the provision that Blake feels uncertain about his capacity to adopt not just the voice but also the activity of the prophet, and if we remember that this activity has relevance to the political realities of England in the 1790s, we can go some way with Bloom's reading.

Some way: but not so far as saying that '*the* precursor-text' (emphasis added) for Blake's 'London' is Ezekiel 9.[22] Given the multiple and complex nature of influence, it's hard to believe that anyone can seriously suggest that a poem only has *one* precursor text. Such an idea is certain to be wrong, even where one text is openly attempting to comment on only one other. The issues are complex. But, as for 'London', one might for instance note the obvious fact that Ezekiel didn't write *songs*. The whole tradition of folksong and ballad is clearly present, and perhaps it won't seem too banal merely to mention the fact. More germane to our discussion of Ezekiel is the fact that the word 'mark' figures in two other biblical texts which would be known to Blake. The phrases are noted by E.P. Thompson: 'the mark of the beast' (Revelation 13:16–17) and 'the mark of Cain' (Genesis 4:15). Thompson notes that the mark of Cain could carry the ambivalence that 'men' are 'both agents and patients, culprits and victims', since 'in Blake's Christian dialectic the mark of Cain could stand simultaneously as a sign of sin and a sign of its forgiveness'.[23] This interpretation would square with the ambivalent view of the speaker.

And Thompson notes that the 'more radical the audience, the more preoccupied it will have been' with Revelation 13:[24]

> And he causeth all, both small and great, rich and poor, free and bond, to receive a mark in their right hand, or in their foreheads:
> And that no man might buy or sell, says he that had the mark, or the name of the beast, or the number of his name.

Of course, radical Dissenters had always associated the Great Beast – the Antichrist – with Priest and King. There is a naturalness about a reading which states that 'London' shows that we all bear the mark of the tyrannies of Priest and King. This is clearly another 'precursor-text'. But, in order to accept it, do we have to say, with Thompson, that despite 'superficial verbal similarities' we should reject the allusion to Ezekiel suggested by Bloom? Why should we do this? Apart from the fact that the 'superficiality' of these verbal similarities is arguable, and that Blake knew his Ezekiel extremely well, why in principle should we reject Ezekiel? Because Thompson would feel that he was involving Blake and himself in a contradiction: to wit, the statement that the speaker and the people both were and were not damned, at the same time.

But this contradiction is in the poem. And there's no reason why it shouldn't be. Blake is simultaneously attracted by the radical view of State versus People, and by the sterner view, for which there was also scriptural warrant, of a whole people accursed. More interesting than trying to even out the contradictions in Blake's texts is the attempt to describe and explain them. The explanation lies in the curious ideological conjuncture which Blake represents, one which revealed to him his dependence on prior and contradictory discourses, so that, even while suggesting a firm, radical course of action, he was aware of his own dependence on conventions and modes of expression which seemed tainted. This was the consequence of coming from a radical Christian background in an age of radical rationalism: the difficulty of reconciling elements in his inheritance with more modern modes of thought and feeling made him acutely aware of differing conventions.

V

The phrase 'contrary states' implies that Innocence and Experience show mutually exclusive points of view: what one sees, the other doesn't. The notion of contraries, derived by Blake from Boehme, has its roots in the Jewish Kabbalistic conception that there were two aspects of God: one merciful, the other wrathful. Christians tended to associate these aspects with Christ and God the Father respectively. For a Behmenist, as Blake in a sense was, such a concept would naturally imply two differing points of view on earth, as well as in heaven. It is fascinating to note that John Byrom, a Behmenist, and near-contemporary of Blake's, had written a parody of Isaac Watts, 'The Potter and his Clay', showing a wrathful God, and had followed this by another hymn, 'The Contrast', showing a merciful one.

III

May not the sov'reign Lord on high
Dispense his Favours as he will?
Chuse some to Life, while others die,
And yet be just and gracious still?

IV

What if, to make his Terror known,
He lets his patience long endure,
   Suff'ring vile Rebels to go on,
And seal their own Destruction sure?
(From 'The Potter and his Clay')

III

This gracious sov'reign Lord on high,
By his eternal Word and Voice,
   Chose *all* to live, and *none* to die,
Nor will he *ever* change his Choice.

IV

Not by *his* Will, but by their *own*,
Vile Rebels break his righteous Laws;
   And make the Terror to be known
Of which they are *themselves* the cause.
(From 'The Contrast')[25]

The last stanza quoted includes the Blakean notion that God only seems to be made of pure terror to those who themselves cannot feel love and mercy.

In a more subtle way Blake's 'The Lamb' and 'The Tyger' also show the two sides of God. One is the emblem of the God visible to Innocence, the other that of the God visible to Experience. For, in asking 'Little Lamb who made thee' and, of the Tyger, 'Did he who made the Lamb make thee?', Blake is really asking, 'Do these creatures express aspects of the Divine, and thus of Humanity also (since God resides "in the human breast")?' Critics and readers generally have no problem with 'The Lamb', whether or not they think that the view of the divine humanity it represents is limited. But when they come to 'The Tyger' they are less sure.[26] The idea that the Tyger is wholly bad can be rejected as obtuse. According to the word of the Bible God made all the beasts, and Blake would interpret this in the 'spiritual sense' as meaning that the whole universe, including the Tyger, expresses the divine. But, if there were any doubt, one need only turn the *The Marriage of Heaven and Hell*, where one reads that 'The tygers of wrath are wiser than the horses of instruction' and that 'The wrath of the lion is the wisdom of god'. 'Energy' is celebrated in *The Marriage*, and it may take the form of honest anger, as opposed to the dissimulating humility of the hypocrite:

> Now the sneaking serpent walks
> In mild humility.
> And the just man rages in the wilds
> Where lions roam.

> (pl. 2, E33/K149)

The emblem of the Tyger is a characteristically salient grafting of one tradition onto another: the Tyger is the wrathful side of God, as seen in the Kabbalist and Behmenist tradition. But at the same time it is the sublime terror of pre-Romantic and Romantic art and aesthetics: it expresses the wild energies celebrated in different style by the paintings of Stubbs. In the early 1790s that wrath and that energy were felt by radicals to have found expression in the French Revolution, whose violence Blake would not, at the time, unequivocally condemn.

Not unequivocally. But equivocation is surely present in 'The Tyger'. The terms in which the creation of the beast is described are those of a harsh manufacture:

> And what shoulder, & what art,
> Could twist the sinews of thy heart?
> And when thy heart began to beat,
> What dread hand? & what dread feet?

> What the hammer? what the chain,
> In what furnace was thy brain?
> What the anvil? what dread grasp,
> Dare its deadly terrors clasp!

> (E24–5/K214)

The 'raw materials' of which the Tyger is made are natural;
the second stanza describes natural elements which are
'seized' and transmuted by the creator:

> In what distant deeps or skies.
> Burnt the fire of thine eyes?
> On what wings dare he aspire?
> What the hand, dare sieze the fire?

The fire in the Tyger's eyes is treated as the essence of
Tyger, to be given body in the manufacturing-process
which follows. It is a natural fire, but one which seems to
remember its heavenly home. The manufacture is violent
and harsh. And that violence and harshness are mirrored in
the creation, which seems to be inhuman and pitiless – it is
as if a monster were being created: 'And when thy heart
began to beat, / What dread hand? & what dread feet?' An
effect as of Frankenstein is achieved by a gradual progression:
from the sense of natural forces as raw material (the fire in
the eyes) to specific organs being manipulated ('twisting'
the 'sinews of the heart') to the image of manufacture
('hammer', 'chain', 'furnace' and 'anvil').

At one level this can be seen as related to Blake's
insistence that Nature does not exist for humanity except as
it is transformed, whether by labour or by imagination
('Where man is not nature is barren' – *MHH*, pl. 10). And
for Blake labour is imaginative, and imagination demands
labour, so that the two terms have only a relative
distinctness. Yet the labour here is harsh, terrifying and
narrow. For the creation of the Tyger demands a kinship
with it. When the poem asks, 'What the hand, dare sieze
the fire?' and 'what shoulder, & what art, / Could twist the
sinews of thy heart?', it implies that only the hand and
shoulder of somebody who contained that fiery essence of
tyger could create such a beast. And yet the beast, merely
by virtue of being a beast, represents something less than a
full humanity, and the images of manufacture also imply
this. So that the creator becomes something less than fully
human.

The poem is a remote comment on both the Industrial Revolution and the political revolutions which it seemed likely would accompany it. The Tyger represents, at one and the same time, a natural energy, and something defined by a harsh mechanical process. It can therefore act as a symbol for the position of the emerging industrial proletariat, a symbol which Blake attempts to define in terms of the 'organic' refined and narrowed by the 'mechanical'. This transition, though it does narrow, also lends terrifying power. Blake was inclined both to approve that power, as necessary to the destruction of the old society, and to fear the consequences of its limited nature, as he saw it. For, separated from love and innocence, how could it possibly build the new society he hoped for?

The creator of the Tyger, who is like his creation, also follows the same process of narrowing: from being fit to seize the sublime fire which goes into the making of the Tyger's eyes, he becomes an alienated labourer. One way of looking at this process is to see it as a 'fall', analogous to the idea of a fall from the spiritual world into Nature: in this respect the poem anticipates Blake's myth of creation-as-fall. But the sublime beauty of the Tyger suggests that only in partial and limited forms could anything exist, just as one could only believe anything by partial and prejudiced 'imposition'. But this dubiety is not resolved: the question whether form is expressive or limiting remains a question, though a profoundly troubling one. Blake's punctuation is always worth examining: although 'The Lamb' and 'The Tyger' ask a similar question, only 'The Tyger' is punctuated with question marks: 'Little Lamb who made thee', without a question mark, expects a foregone conclusion. But the insistent questions of 'The Tyger' are appropriately punctuated, and express a contrasting doubtfulness. Nevertheless, Blake's ambivalence about form does, as we have seen, express itself in *Innocence* as well as *Experience*. Indeed, the more one reads the combined book, *Songs of Innocence and of Experience*, the more this ambivalence conditions one's response.

3 Unsteady States:
Songs of Innocence and of Experience

We have seen that both *Songs of Innocence* and *Songs of Experience* contain poems that are ironic about the limitations of the represented speaker, and about their own means of expression. One way in which they suggest this irony is by implying the perspective of the opposing state. Thus 'The Chimney Sweeper' hints at the perspective of *Experience*. It's easy to see this stratagem at work in some of the songs. The *Innocence* 'Holy Thursday' provides a case almost exactly parallel with that of 'The Chimney Sweeper': one reading is usually sufficient to disturb our confidence in *Innocence*.

> Twas on a Holy Thursday their innocent faces clean
> The children walking two & two in red & blue & green
> Grey headed beadles walkd before with wands as white as snow
> Till into the high dome of Pauls they like Thames waters flow
>
> O what a multitude they seemd these flowers of London town
> Seated in companies they sit with radiance all their own
> The hum of multitudes was there but multitudes of lambs
> Thousands of little boys & girls raising their innocent hands

Now like a mighty wind they raise to heaven the voice
    of song
Or like harmonious thunderings the seats of heaven
    among
Beneath them sit the aged men wise guardians of the
    poor
Then cherish pity, lest you drive an angel from your
    door

                         (E13/K121–2)

Holy Thursday is here Ascension Day, when six thousand
or so children from London charity schools would go to St
Paul's to listen to a sermon and sing hymns in front of their
benefactors, who were presumably pleased to be thanked so
ostentatiously in the presence of the Almighty. Blake's
irony is plain in the sly platitude of the last line. And one is
alerted on reading this, if not before, to the regimentation of
the children by the hoary discipline of 'grey headed
beadles' with 'wands as white as snow', ready to freeze the
energies of youth.

    It's easy to see irony in 'Holy Thursday'. But other songs
may seem too fragile to bear this burden. Nevertheless,
once one is aware of the possibility, even the most
innocuous-seeming lyric can be seen to contain implications
that are hard to ignore. We have already suggested that
there are references to sexuality in 'The Blossom' which are
beyond the ken of the imputed speaker. And we have also
suggested that those Songs of Innocence, such as 'Night',
'The Little Boy Found' or 'A Dream', which involve a
comforting end to a disturbing story, may be regarded as
'fairy tales' in the colloquial sense.

    But there are other songs which suggest a limitation on
the speaker:

Can I see anothers woe,
And not be in sorrow too.
Can I see anothers grief,
And not seek for kind relief.

Can I see a falling tear,
And not feel my sorrows share,
Can a father see his child,
Weep, nor be with sorrow fill'd.

Can a mother sit and hear,
An infant groan an infant fear –
No no never can it be.
Never never can it be.

                                      (E17/K122–3)

The insistent rejection of the idea that such a mother could exist puts the speaker's view in question – and with reason.

Other Songs of Innocence seem to be devoid of any internal irony. It is hard to find anything but the most ingenuous celebration of childish joy in 'Laughing Song' or 'Nurse's Song':

Well well go & play till the light fades away
And then go home to bed
The little ones leaped & shouted & laugh'd
And all the hills ecchoed

                          ('Nurse's Song', E15/K121)

One might ask whether the forecast that the light will fade away, and the gentle injunction to go home to bed, are ominous: such doubts Blake sows in the reader's mind. But it seems impossible to settle this question, and one is inclined to put the main stress on the innocently joyful character of the song. Does this mean that our ironic readings of some of the *Innocence* songs must founder? Not at all. We are not trying to uncover the pure essence of Blakean Innocence. In the nature of texts, this could not exist. Blake did not succeed in creating a uniform Innocence, if that is what he wanted to do. It may be doubted whether writers ever succeed in creating uniformity. So there are some songs which reveal, more or less directly, the limitations of speakers, and others which seem like pure celebrations. Of course, the latter can be read ironically in the context of *Innocence* as a whole. But to insist on this is to erect another critical idol. We may remain as uncertain as Blake undoubtedly was. Indeed, to oscillate between two readings, one ironic and the other 'straight', may be the fullest response one can have to these poems.

This uncertainty is pointed up by Blake's indecision about where to place some of the songs: four of the Songs of Experience originally appeared in *Songs of Innocence*: 'The Little Girl Lost', 'The Little Girl Found', 'The School Boy' and 'The Voice of the Ancient Bard'. And indeed, it's possible to wonder at first why some of them were moved. 'The Little Girl Lost' and 'Found' are a pair of 'fairy-tale' poems (E20–3/K112–15: Keynes keeps them in *Innocence* in his edition) with a basic structure not unlike that of 'The Little Boy Lost' and 'Found' of *Innocence*. The little girl, Lyca, is a maiden 'Seven summers old' who wanders away from her parents and becomes 'Lost in desert wild'. She is found by leopards, 'tygers' and lions, who guard her and care for her. Her parents, meanwhile, have set out to find her and finally encounter a 'couching lion' who turns out to be 'A spirit arm'd in gold'. He leads them to his 'palace', where they find 'their sleeping child, / Among tygers wild'. The poem ends,

> To this day they dwell
> In a lonely dell
> Nor fear the wolvish howl,
> Nor the lions growl.

Like some songs that remain in *innocence* 'A Little Girl Lost' contains hints of sexuality. On the first plate we see, to the right of the text, the picture of a girl being embraced by a youth in a frankly sexual manner. The girl is obviously older than seven years. But perhaps she is not Lyca. On the next plate the same girl, to judge by the colour of her dress and hair, is seen lying on the forest floor. This does seem to identify her with the lost Lyca. In the third plate a naked girl, whose body is clearly more than seven years old, is seen lying asleep in the company of a lion and lioness. It seems that the seven years may be symbolic, rather than literal. If so, they would be likely to represent the seven days of creation, and would symbolize the fact that Lyca had passed beyond the material world: that is, according to Blake's revision of traditional symbolism, she had passed beyond the dualism of mind and body, and the shame that attends it. Hence the invocation of sexuality, which can also be seen in the text:

> Leopards, tygers play,
> Round her as she lay;
> While the lion old,
> Bow'd his mane of gold.

> And her bosom lick,
> And upon her neck,
> From his eyes of flame,
> Ruby tears there came;

> While the lioness,
> Loos'd her slender dress,
> And naked they convey'd
> To caves the sleeping maid.

(E21/K113)

Just as Lyca learns to accept sexuality, she learns to accept wrath and the other 'energies' of Experience: 'Nor fear the wolvish howl, / Nor the lions growl'.

It's clear now why Blake moved these poems out of *Innocence*: they recommend the path through Experience, through its sublime but dangerous energies. On the other hand, they don't even sit all that easily with some of the other Songs of Experience, either. For, whereas Lyca retains love and innocence, even while learning to encompass the dangers of Experience, many of the speakers in this state appear to have lost these qualities. In this way 'The Little Girl Lost' and 'Found' point the way forward out of Experience towards some accommodation of the two contraries: this accommodation is the discovery of a true innocence, energetic and undeceived. A similar perspective is offered by 'The Voice of the Ancient Bard', which Blake usually placed at, or near, the end of *Songs of Experience*, once he had moved it from *Innocence*:

> Youth of delight come hither:
> And see the opening morn,
> Image of truth new born.
> Doubt is fled & clouds of reason,
> Dark disputes & artful teazing.
>
> (E31/K126: again Keynes keeps
> the earlier position in *Innocence*)

Of course, if Blake had left these poems in *Innocence* critics would have had no problem inventing arguments for why they were most fittingly placed there. And indeed one could find quite good arguments of this type: the notion of 'true innocence' would be seen as merely another inflection of the notion of Innocence in general. The fundamental instability of the contraries makes this possible. It arises from the fact that both *Innocence* and *Experience* are attempts to suggest the possibilities for, and the limitations on, 'innocence' (a happy, loving, communal state) in a world where limits are inevitable. In *Innocence* the limits tend to go unrecognized; in *Experience* they tend to be recognized and challenged: the leafy and the leafless frame. But both *Innocence* and *Experience* are difficult 'stabs' at 'true innocence', with an awareness of the difficulties built in.

It's perhaps for this reason that many of the Songs of Experience sound quite as much like children's songs as do most of the Songs of Innocence. Or to put it another way: it's not so much that *Innocence* is about childhood and *Experience* about adulthood, as that childhood is important to the description of innocence, and thus of 'true innocence'. Therefore parts of *Songs of Experience* are about children and their treatment, or sound like children's songs.

Consider 'The Tyger': the questions asked in it are

clearly comparable to the sublime questions with which
God interrogates Job, as here:

> Wilt thou hunt the prey for the lion?
> or fill the appetite of the young lions?

> Canst thou bind the unicorn with his
> band in the furrow? or will he harrow
> the valleys after thee?

> Hast thou given the horse strength?
> hast thou clothed his neck with thunder?
>
> (Job 38:39; 39:10, 19)

Blake often imitates these questions, as at the end of *The
Book of Thel*. The Book of Job was regarded at this time as
one of the most 'sublime' books of the Bible: Burke, for
instance, mentions it in his *Enquiry*. The questions in 'The
Tyger' are intended to imply the awful and sublime
mystery of the divine. But the song-like metre detracts to
some extent from the impression of Old Testament
sublimity. As with many song and ballad metres, its effect
can vary with different readings. It is appropriately
insistent and heavy: three trochees followed by one strong
stress (—u/—u/—u/—). But, even so, it might seem
sufficiently singing to be treated as a children's song or
hymn – as, indeed, it is treated. When read in this way, the
questions become wondering and innocent – not unlike
those in the 'contrary' poem, 'The Lamb'. It's intriguing to
note that the metre of 'The Lamb' (three trochees per line)
only differs by the absence of the heavy stress at the end of
the line in 'The Tyger' – as if Blake, while giving a clear
metrical pointer to the contrast between the two emblems,
was also giving a metrical hint of the similarity in the
represented attitude of the speaker. If 'The Tyger' in some
respects verges on being a Song of Innocence, this might
explain why the illumination makes that savage beast look
like a cuddly toy – a fact which has vexed and perplexed
many an earnest critic. Of course there is another explanation: Blake was sometimes a very inept draughtsman.

But rare is the 'Blakean' who could commit to print such an infringement of the rules of critical hagiolatry (which is not to say that doubts can't be raised about the meaning of 'ineptitude' in drawing). Probably to plump confidently for either of these views of the illumination is to succumb to the fallacy of absolute critical certitude.

Despite the many clear differences in style between most of the *Innocence* and most of the *Experience* songs, it is nevertheless true that many of the Songs of Experience are about children, or imply a child narrator. The question posed by *Songs of Innocence and of Experience* as a whole is: what is true innocence? And this true innocence cannot be spoken of in the terms set by most of the poems in either of the two series. Blake was not sufficiently confident that it was possible to conceive of a world or a discourse without limitation and 'imposition', which is what true innocence would mean.

II

This indecision about whether form is limiting or liberating, and the implication that perhaps it is both, clearly reflects on Blake's own role as a creator of poetic form. His doubts about this role are strikingly expressed in the 'Introduction' to *Experience*, which is about the activity of a 'Bard':

Hear the voice of the Bard!
Who Present, Past, & Future sees
Whose ears have heard,
The Holy Word,
That walk'd among the ancient trees.

Calling the lapsed Soul
And weeping in the evening dew:
That might controll,
The starry pole;
And fallen fallen light renew!

O Earth O Earth return!
Arise from out the dewy grass;
Night is worn,
And the morn
Rises from the slumberous mass.

Turn away no more:
Why wilt thou turn away
The starry floor
The watry shore
Is giv'n thee till the break of day.

(E18/K210)

There is an obvious ambiguity here, in that the address to
'Earth' in stanzas 3 and 4 could either be the original
sentiments of the Bard; or else a form of words prompted by
the 'Holy Word' and derivative from it – possibly even
reported speech, in which case the Bard is merely speaking
from 'Dictation', as Blake once claimed that he himself
wrote (letter to Butts, 25 Apr. 1803, E729/K823), a
paradoxical claim for someone who prized 'original' genius.
Robert F. Gleckner says that there are 'two voices' in this
poem, that of the Bard and that of the Holy Word: the Bard
is inspired, the Holy Word is the dead letter of God the
Father.[1] This is a handy formulation. But it remains open
to misunderstanding. It fails to explain the relationship
between the two voices. In particular it fails to explain how
it is that the Bard should be reporting, however indirectly,
sentiments which can be attributed to a tyrannical deity.
Better to say that the poem is completely ambiguous from
beginning to end. For example, we are told that the Bard
sees 'Present, Past, & Future'. This refers to his prophetic
faculty, for in Blake's time the theory was that ancient
bards had been regarded as prophets, and by the same
token that the Hebrew prophets had been bards – a fairly
accurate theory, in fact.[2] But one could see this bard either
as liberated from the bonds of time, and thus from
distinctions of present, past and future; or else as the kind of
prophet who divides and measures time, thus limiting

imagination. He has given ear to the Holy Word: this could mean that he is a passive recipient of the words of a law-giving deity; or else that he is inspired. When the Bard promises that the Soul 'might controll / The starry pole' (that is, the zenith of the heavens, covered with stars, including the Pole Star) this could mean that she can regain control over Destiny (the stars referring to astrology); or else that she herself may exercise the dominion of the tyrannical stars – may control the Destiny of others.

The Bard who merely reports the sentiments of the Holy Word is the prophet-turned-priest. He has turned the living word of inspiration into the dead letter of the law. He succumbs to influence as constraint, as limitation. The Bard as inspired poet–prophet is he whose word derives from living experience – though it is notable that even when regarded in this light his message cannot but seem in some sense derivative, since he has 'heard, / The Holy Word' too. In this aspect, then, influence, though still unavoidable, is enlisted in the cause of inspiration. In this poem, then, Blake inscribes his doubts about whether form is limiting or expressive in words that leave it open to doubt whether he regards it as being one or the other. The idea of 'two voices' tends to obscure the fact that Blake conceives of these two aspects of form as so closely allied that they can be spoken of together by an ambiguous use of one form of words. The two aspects of the Bard correspond to a curious ambiguity in Blake's use of a key term of his: the 'bound' (or the 'bounded'), clearly a word implying limitation.

4   The Ambiguity of Bound:
There is No Natural Religion (*c*.1788), *Europe* (1794)

I

Most of Blake's works, including the *Songs*, are colour-printed by a peculiar method of relief etching involving printing from the raised parts of the surface of engraved copper plates. The first works he produced in this idiosyncratic method were the three texts sometimes known as 'the early tractates': *All Religions are One*; and *There is No Natural Religion*, in two series, (a) and (b). They date from about 1788, that is to say from a period when presumably he had either completed, or was in the process of completing, most of the Songs of Innocence. And it seems likely that the tractates were important to him, since they were the first works he printed by this method. Because they date from just before the completion of *Songs of Innocence* they are likely to be relevant to a study of the *Songs*. And this is indeed so. But in fact they also provide clues to the understanding of all of Blake's work, almost as if he were issuing a prospectus. They take the form of terse, logical arguments for Blake's prophetic stance, and against the 'philosophy of the five senses', as he called the reigning empiricism (the doctrine that knowledge is ultimately derived from simple sensory experience). They are also very abstract, but this is a quality they share with much of Blake's poetry.

We shall look here mainly at *There is No Natural Religion* (a) and (b), with just a glance at *All Religions are One*. Perhaps the first question to ask is: 'What is "Natural Religion"?'

Liberal religious thinking in the eighteenth century comprised many shades of opinion. What was common to most forms of liberal, non-atheist thought was the belief that the universe gives evidence of creation to a rational mind. Natural Religion (or 'Deism', a term Blake often used for it) found nothing 'unreasonable' in the Christian revelation. All truths, great and small, were accessible to Reason, which was the universal property of all human beings. This view naturally tended to make God look like the Great Reason, and religions essentially like the moral behaviour of all reasonable people. All this seemed to the more thorough-going thinkers of the Enlightenment (as this period came to be called) a veritably marvellous reduction of the diversity of religious custom, Christian and non-Christian, to one valid principle: Reason sloughed of the richness of religious diversity (all that 'superstition') and the pretensions of theological debate at one end of the same time. So it seemed to Voltaire:

> Let not the trifling difference between the vestments that cover our weak bodies, between our defective languages, our ridiculous customs, our numerous imperfect laws, our idle opinions, our several conditions, so disproportionate in our eyes, and so equal in thine; let not the little shades of rank or party, which distinguish the several atoms called men, be the signals of hatred and persecution! May those who celebrate thy name by wax light at noon-day, tolerate such as are content with the light of the sun. Let not those who put on a white linen surplice to tell us we must love thee, hold in detestation such as preach the same doctrine in a cloak of black woollen. May it be the same thing to adore thee in a jargon taken from an ancient language, as in a similar jargon formed on a modern one.[1]

Similar sentiments, not always so fervently expressed, can be found throughout Voltaire's works. Blake's assaults on Natural Religion and 'Voltaire and Rousseau' are directed against this way of thinking.

This analytical reduction of the diversity of world religions echoes more general scientific and philosophical procedures encouraged by the Enlightenment: the 'discursive form of knowledge always resembles a reduction; it proceeds from the complex to the simple, from apparent diversity to its basic identity'.[2] Or as Horkheimer and Adorno put it, in *Dialectic of Enlightenment*, such thinking makes 'the dissimilar comparable by reducing it to abstract quantities' (New York, 1972, p. 7).

Blake also proclaims that 'All Religions are One'. But, as he points out in the tractate of that name, the unity of religions for him consists in their being 'derived from each Nations different reception of the Poetic Genius which is every where call'd the Spirit of Prophecy' (E1/K98). In other words, the unity of religions is based on Imagination, not on Reason. This is a unity which can only ensure the diversity of religious forms: Blake is appreciative of the 'different reception' accorded by each nation. When he writes about the 'patriarchates of Asia' it is with a sense of richness and vitality lost:

> The two Pictures of Nelson and Pitt are compositions of a mythological cast, similar to those Apotheoses of Persian, Hindoo, and Egyptian Antiquity, which are still preserved on rude monuments, being copies from some stupendous originals now lost or perhaps buried till some happier age.
>
> (*A Descriptive Catalogue*, 1809, E530–1/K565)

The function of Persians, Hindus and other orientals is very different in the polemics of the Enlightenment, where we are all identical under the 'vestments', to pick up an interesting word from Voltaire. Montesquieu's *Lettres persanes* or Goldsmith's *Citizen of the World* are intended to show that reasonable people are the same everywhere, and also that much that was distinctive about European culture was irrational and absurd, and could be shown to be so through the eyes of an outsider. But for Blake human identity resides in difference, in the famous 'minute particulars' – in different 'vestments', if you like.

Blake's tractates *There is No Natural Religion* (a) and (b) are intended to prove the necessity of Imagination (the 'Poetic Genius') to any kind of knowledge. He regards it as the true cognitive faculty. It brings about all advances in knowledge, even scientific knowledge, which for him is not something essentially uniform and immutable, but has to be unveiled as part of the historical process: 'Reason or the ratio of all we have already known. is not the same that it shall be when we know more' (E2/K97).[3]

II

In the first series of *There is No Natural Religion* Blake concentrates on the limitations of the 'natural man', who is capable of seeing the truths of Natural Religion:

The Argument. Man has no notion of moral fitness but from Education. Naturally he is only a natural organ subject to Sense.

I   Man cannot naturally Perceive. but through his natural or bodily organs

II   Man by his reasoning power. can only compare & judge of what he has already perciev'd

III From a perception of only 3 senses or 3 elements none could deduce a fourth or fifth

IV None could have other than natural or organic thoughts if he had none but organic perceptions

V   Mans desires are limited by his perceptions. none can desire what he has not perciev'd

VI The desires & perceptions of man untaught by any thing but organs of sense, must be limited to objects of sense. (E2/K97)

Blake accepts St Paul's doctrine that 'the natural man receiveth not the things of the spirit' (1 Corinthians 2:14). And it's plain from his annotations of Swedenborg that he also accepts the latter's elaboration of this theme. Thus: 'Observe the distinction here between Natural & Spiritual as seen by Man . . . Man may comprehend [The Divine]. but not the natural or external man' (E603/K90). But Blake goes beyond this in extending the term 'natural' to empiricist thinking. His tactic, in the first series, is to accept a thorough-going empiricism for the natural man. It's as if he should say, 'I accept your conclusions as to the foundations of human knowledge, but only for that small portion of humanity I call "natural".' The second aphorism, for instance, speaks directly to the concise definition of knowledge given by John Locke, the father of British empiricism:

> *Knowledge* then seems to me to be nothing but *the perception of the connexion and agreement, or disagreement and repugnancy of any of our ideas*. In this alone it consists. Where this perception is, there is knowledge; and where it is not, there, though we may fancy, guess, or believe, yet we always come short of knowledge. (*Essay concerning Human Understanding*, IV.i.2)

There is also a reference to Bacon's scientific method of accumulating data for comparison, of which Locke's definition is a theoretical justification.

The third aphorism is particularly interesting: 'From a perception of only 3 senses or 3 elements none could deduce a fourth or fifth'. This refers to a tradition of speculation on the senses initiated by William Molyneux (1656–98) of Trinity College, Dublin. What came to be known as 'Molyneux's problem' gained celebrity from its use by Locke in his chapter 'Of Perception' (*Essay*, II.ix.8). Molyneux's question (there quoted in full) was: Would a man born blind be able at once, if he were given his sight back, to distinguish between a cube and a sphere, say, given that he had already learnt to distinguish them by touch? His answer was, No: the blind man would have to learn to interpret visual sense data from scratch (so to speak) by experiencing the agreement of sight and touch. Locke was of the same opinion.

It was left to Berkeley to express the full implications of this conclusion in the *Essay towards a New Theory of Vision* (1709), where he says it is certain that 'the ideas intromitted by each sense are widely different, and distinct from each other' (section XLVI), and, more extremely, 'the ideas which constitute the tangible earth and man, are entirely different from those which constitute the visible earth and man' (section CII). The five senses tended by some to be regarded as an almost arbitrary assortment of isolated and distinct 'windows' on the world. Thus, Fontenelle, in *A Conversation on the Plurality of Worlds* (1st edn Paris, 1686; this translation London, 1777) is driven to fantastic speculation of this kind:

> Here it is thought we want a sixth sense, that would teach us many things, of which we are now ignorant; this sixth sense is apparently in another world, where they want one of the five which we enjoy; nay, perhaps there is a much greater number of senses, but in the partition which we have made of them with the inhabitants of the other planets, there are but five fallen to our share, with which we are well contented for want of being acquainted with the rest: Our sciences have *bounds*, which the wit of man could never pass. (p. 78; emphasis added)

Blake had probably read this translation[4] But on the subject of the senses alone, it is noteworthy that he associates the idea of 'numerous senses' with a transcendence of the bounds of the Philosophy of the Five Senses: 'The ancient Poets animated all sensible objects with Gods or Geniuses, calling them by the names and adorning them with the properties of woods, rivers, mountains, lakes, cities, nations, and whatever their enlarged & numerous senses could percieve,' (*MHH*, pl. 11, E38/K153). In *The*

First Book of Urizen (1794) the Eternals are similarly endowed:

> Earth was not: nor globes of attraction
> The will of the Immortal expanded
> Or contracted his all flexible senses.
> Death was not, but eternal life sprung
> > (3:36–9, E71/K153)

The isolation of each sense is described in *Europe* (1794):

> Five windows light the cavern'd Man; thro' one he
> > breathes the air;
> Thro' one, hears music of the spheres; thro' one, the
> > eternal vine
> Flourishes, that he may recieve the grapes; thro' one
> > can look.
> And see small portions of the eternal world that ever
> > groweth;
> Thro' one, himself pass out what time he please, but
> > he will not . . .
> > (*Europe*, iii:1–5, E60/K237)

In the aphorism under discussion Blake is using our ignorance of other possible senses as a metaphor for knowledge not given by sense. Exactly the same device had been used satirically by Voltaire, in a Supplement to *The Ignorant Philosopher*, in which some blind people elect 'professors' of sight from among themselves (the satire is clearly aimed at theologians).

Blake isn't speculating on the possibility that the Poetic Genius would literally reveal a sixth or seventh sense. Rather, he is emphasizing the limitations of the senses, and, against Voltaire, arguing for the importance of the imagination: 'If it were not for the Poetic or Prophetic character the Philosophic & Experimental would soon be at the ratio of all things, & stand still unable to do other than repeat the same dull round over again'.

Yet paradoxically, even by allowing that a 'natural man' is indeed limited to five senses, unless aided by imagination,

Blake is giving qualified assent to the ideas of the empiricist philosophers. This fact can help to illustrate his curious, ambivalent relationship to the Enlightenment philosophers, which we touched on in our first chapter. Consider the 'Argument' of *There is No Natural Religion* (a). Its subject is Education (a topic relevant to the study of the *Songs* – 'The School Boy' and 'Holy Thursday', for instance). The subjection of youthful inspiration to dead, systematic book-learning, as he thought of it, seemed useless to Blake. The theme appears very clearly, for instance, in a watercolour, *Age Teaching Youth* (*c.* 1785–90, Tate Gallery). An old man holds out an open book, with an almost admonitory gesture, to a child who, though reading, points to the sky, as if to indicate another source of wisdom. A boy in the foreground is bent over a book: he wears a garment decorated with a foliate pattern, associating him with a restricted kind of innocence which has become bound to the world of Nature.

The Argument of *No Natural Religion* (a) is a truncated statement of fashionable Rousseauesque views on education – views which Blake didn't hold. He particularly has in mind Mary Wollstonecraft's *Original Stories From Real Life* (1788). The pertinent passage comes from her introduction:

> The way to render instruction most useful cannot always be adopted; knowledge should be gradually imparted, and flow more from example than teaching: example directly addresses the senses, the first *inlets* to the heart; and the improvement of those instruments of the understanding is the object education should have constantly in view, and over which we have most power.[5] (Emphasis added)

In *The Marriage of Heaven and Hell* Blake actually refers to the senses as 'inlets', as Wollstonecraft does above: 'Man has no Body distinct from his Soul for that calld Body is a portion of Soul discernd by the five Senses. the chief inlets of Soul in this age' (pl. 4, E34/K149). The combination of the subjects of sensory experience and education in both

Original Stories and *The Marriage*, together with the fact that
Blake uses the word 'inlet' himself, make it very likely that
he is commenting on the Wollstonecraft passage. But, in
any case, 'inlet' was a fairly common word in empiricist
discussion of the senses. And here again we have Blake
allowing a certain importance to empiricist ideas: the
'inlets' are limited, but they are the *chief* inlets of 'Soul'. In
other words they are amongst those typically Blakean
entities: vehicles which both obstruct and permit, like
'states'.

But to return to the Argument: it might seem that the
idea of repressive book-learning has little to do with the
emphasis on the senses promoted by Wollstonecraft. Why,
for instance, does Blake depict a harmful bookishness in his
illumination to this aphorism? A sitting woman seems to be
holding a tablet, and a girl to be standing holding a book
(see *IB* 28). The aphorism itself is the beginning of an
argument against education through the *senses*, seemingly
the opposite of the *book*.

Rousseau was quite extreme in his proposals for change
in education. There was only one book in Emile's library –
Robinson Crusoe, a choice in itself significant of the emergent
bourgeois world view, and its celebration of the isolated,
untrammelled self:

> Reading is a vexation to children, and yet it is the only
> occupation they are usually employed in. Emilius will
> hardly know what a book is at twelve years of age: but
> you will say, he ought surely to learn to read, at least.
> Yet, he shall learn to read when reading will be of any
> use to him; till then it is good for nothing but to
> disgust and fatigue him.[6]

Now Blake certainly agrees with the mistrust of book-
learning. So his illustration to the aphorism presumably
suggests that Rousseau's 'education through the senses' is
already inscribed with deadly system. For, of course, he
does not find the 'natural' life of the senses essentially
human. Empiricist philosophies are, to him, an obstruction

of what he takes to be the true essence: Imagination. The illustration, therefore, is a *deconstruction*, in the strictest sense, of Rousseau. The privileged term in Rousseau, 'senses', is set against the secondary one, 'letter' or 'book'. But Blake indicates that the idea of a free, unspoilt life of the senses is as much a cultural construct as is any book. For him, this idea of the senses is an obstruction to the Imagination, as is enslavement to books. This wariness about the basis of liberal educational ideas may help to explain why some of the *Songs*, such as 'Infant Joy', which at first glance may seem to be simple celebrations of childhood, in fact reveal an adult putting supposedly simple words into a child's mouth.

On the other hand Rousseau's belief in the innate goodness of the child, his attack on parental tyranny, and his mistrust of the book, would appeal to Blake's radical-Protestant preferences (the opposition of Spirit and Letter was beloved of Boehme and the antinomians). Likewise the term 'Imagination' can be seen as antinomian 'Revelation' in late eighteenth-century dress. But he could never accept the Enlightenment premise of an intellectual and moral life built up from sensory experience. What one has, then, is a typical piece of grafting. Or, if you like, Blake's works 'pick up' and 'lean on' those features of Enlightenment discourse that consort well with the libertarian, communitarian Christian tradition. The two ideological worlds intensify and qualify each other, but the terms are set by radical Christianity. Blake attempts to suppress and reject those parts of Enlightenment discourse that are clearly rationalist. His ideas were produced by Boehme out of Rousseau.

III

The second series of *There is No Natural Religion* is an answer to the first:

I   Mans perceptions are not *bounded* by organs of

perception. he percieves more than sense (tho' ever so acute) can discover.

II   Reason or the ratio of all we have already known. is not the same that it shall be when we know more. [III lacking]

IV The *bounded* is loathed by its possessor. The same dull round even of a univer[s]e would soon become a mill with complicated wheels.

V   If the many become the same as the few, when possess'd, More! More! is the cry of a mistaken soul, less than All cannot satisfy Man.

VI If any could desire what he is incapable of possessing, despair must be his eternal lot.

VII The desire of Man being Infinite the possession is Infinite & himself Infinite

Application. He who sees the Infinite in all things sees God. He who sees the Ratio only sees himself only. (E2–3/K97–8; emphasis added)

Reason is something that changes 'when we know more'. The cause of our knowing more is the 'Poetic or Phrophetic character' ('Conclusion'), which exhibits itself as a kind of divine restlessness, an endless desire for more, as in the fourth aphorism. The idea of a universe becoming a 'mill with complicated wheels' provides, like other statements of Blake's, a striking analogy with the feelings of the young Goethe and his friends about certain Enlightenment thinkers. They felt as if

> they were walking among countless moving spools and looms in a great factory where the bewilderment produced by the machinery, the incomprehensibility of the complicated interlocking process, and the consideration of all that goes into the production of a piece of cloth, caused them to grow disgusted with the very coats they had on.[7]

It's not simply the mechanical model of the universe and its parts that occasions the loathing, but far more the infection of imagination with a sense of things as mechanism. The world is not only described mechanistically for the purposes of science. It is experienced thus.

This usurpation of the realm of the Poetic Genius by a reductionist model is what most exercises Blake. 'Bacon & Newton & Locke' can hardly be summed up by the triple monster Blake turns them into in his later prophetic books. Nevertheless, this monster is real: the image the eighteenth century had of these thinkers, representing Enlightenment and a new world view. Gerd Buchdahl makes this point well in *The Image of Newton and Locke in the Age of Reason*: 'Of course, relevant here were not so much the details of Newton's and Locke's achievements (often technical, abstruse, even incoherent as they appeared to the ordinary man), but rather the 'image' that the eighteenth century was making for itself of these figures.'[8] The 'image' was equally that of the world these figures were thought to have unveiled.

Blake's answer is to reverse the process: he becomes a 'counter-usurper', as it were: he boldly transposes scientific terms into his own system. How often what Blake borrows (and he borrows much) is tainted, in the ostensible terms of his own philosophy! He wrenches scientific terms into the function of symbols for the imaginative life. This is true of Descarte's 'vortices', which become Blake's 'vortexes' in his later works. And (returning to *No Natural Religion*) it is also true of the 'Infinite' and the 'Ratio': 'He who sees the Infinite in all things sees God. He who sees the Ratio only sees himself only.'

The terms 'Infinite' and 'Ratio' appear elsewhere in Blake's work. They exhibit all his taste for the widely suggestive pun. The 'Infinite' conveys release from the Newtonian absolute Time and Space, which were everywhere and always constant. In Newton's Calculus (or 'Fluctions') the infinite appears only as that which eludes measurement when a quantity is reduced infinitely, or continually augmented to infinity. Between these infinities, to which 'all quantities that begin and cease to be' are always tending, Newton's method allows for an unprecedented exactness in the measurement of motion.

The units of the measurement of motion are called 'ratios': and the prime and ultimate ratios, those ratios with which quantities begin and cease to be, are called 'limits'.[9] The aphorism in question is an ironic transposition of Newton's terms into a context where Blake would see them as having a prophetic function. His 'Infinite' conveys not only what lies beyond the *limits* (or bounds) of Newtonian philosophy, but also the elusive vitality of motion, of which the ratio is both a reduction and an improper image. Such vitality is change in history; in individuals, energy. It escapes the 'horizon' of universal Reason. As Urizen complains,

> I have sought for a joy without pain,
> For a solid without fluctuation
> Why will you die O Eternals?
> Why live in unquenchable burnings?
>   (*Urizen*, 4:10–13, E71/K224)

The same aphorism is illustrated, as Erdman describes, with 'A bearded man on hands and knees' who is 'drawing, on the ground, a triangle which mirrors the shape of his compasses' (*IB* 32). The picture is very similar, in its subject matter, to the large colour print *Newton* (1795) in the Tate Gallery. The compasses in iconography are the symbol of Mathematics, and a pair of compasses, with or without the allegorical figure of Mathematics, often appears in works on the subject of Newton.[10] Voltaire gives prominence to '*Newton's* Compass' in the dedicatory poem to his *Elements of Sir Isaac Newton's Philosophy*.[11] But compasses may be seen as limiting, not just measuring. The limit is that of 'bounded' thought, confined to the measurement of sense data. This idea may be expressed by another meaning of the word 'compass'. Locke speaks of 'the compass of human understanding' (*Essay*, IV.vi.2). Or, more appositely, he claims for his work 'that before we have done, we shall see, that nobody need be afraid, he shall not have scope and compass enough for his thoughts to range in, though they be, as I pretend, confined only to simple *ideas* received from sensation or reflection, and their several combinations' (II.xxii.9).

Another type of horizon and another pair of compasses are associated with a part of geometry that Blake must have known something about: perspective. ('Horizon' is a technical term in perspective for the bound of vision in the optical sense; the mathematical nature of the science of perspective was symbolized by the compasses.) The received wisdom in Blake's time was that perspective was necessary for the correct imitation of Nature in painting. But obviously enslavement to such a goal would seem to Blake like the denial of imagination. And he would dislike the fact that the rigorous use of perspective was an entirely mathematical procedure. The attempt to copy Nature allows 'Mathematic Proportion' to usurp 'Living Proportion' (cf. *Milton*, 5:44,E99/K485). Such an effect in art is analogous to that of Newton's 'fluctions' in the measurement of motion.

All these ideas contribute to the notion of the 'bounded' in aphorisms I and IV, and also to the name of Blake's tyrant–god, Urizen, who wields the compasses in the famous print known as *The Ancient of Days* (in fact the frontispiece to *Europe*). The name 'Urizen' is a pun on 'Your Reason' and the Greek word *horízein*, 'to bound or limit'. The idea of the 'bounded' is essential to Urizen, as it is to the argument of *No Natural Religion*. It's easy to see why. In each case the target is what Blake calls the 'Philosophy of the Five Senses'. The 'natural man', he who does not see that the Poetic Genius is the motive power of Science and Religion alike, is a believer in that philosophy, 'bounded' by organs of perception. For Blake sees empiricism not as one kind of philosophy among many, but as a distillation of error:

Thus the terrible race of Los & Enitharmon gave
Laws & Religions to the sons of Har binding them
   more

And more to Earth: closing and restraining:
Till a Philosophy of Five Senses was complete
Urizen wept & gave it into the hands of Newton &
    Locke

(*Song of Los*, 4:13–17, E68/K246)

IV

But the idea of the 'bounded' represents an acute paradox
in Blake's work. For various inflections of the word 'bound'
may be used entirely approvingly, as well as entirely
pejoratively, depending on their context. We have seen that
'The bounded is loathed by its possessor'. But 'Truth has
bounds. Error none' is an equally characteristic expression
of Blake's philosophy. In what sense may 'bounds' be
desirable?

Blake's graphic works are normally linear in style.
Outline is stressed. In *A Descriptive Catalogue* (1809) he
makes plain his preference for 'firm and determinate
outline':

> The great and golden rule of art, as well as of life, is
> this: That the more distinct, sharp, and wirey the
> *bounding line*, the more perfect the work of art; and the
> less keen and sharp, the greater is the evidence of weak
> imitation, plagiarism, and bungling . . . The want of
> this determinate and bounding form evidences the
> want of idea in the artist's mind, and the pretence of
> the plagiary in all its branches. How do we distinguish
> the oak from the beech, the horse from the ox, but by
> the *bounding outline*? How do we distinguish one face or
> countenance from another, but by the bounding line
> and its infinite inflexions and movements? (E550/
> K585; emphasis added)

There are two ways of distinguishing the bounding-line
here. In the first part of the passage it is something *imposed*
by a strong artist: firm ideas, firm outlines. There is a clear

link here with the ideas of 'imposition' and 'firm perswasion' in *The Marriage*. In the second part of the passage, the bounding-line is the means by which individual identity expresses itself, as in the idea of telling one face from another. But in both these cases the bounding-line is expressive, rather than limiting.

Blake's preference accorded with that of the fashionable Neoclassical school in art. This term might surprise some people, in connection with Blake. But it refers to a fashionable movement in graphic art, sculpture and architecture sometimes called the 'Grecian Revival', and not to the earlier Augustan critical consensus. John Flaxman, the best-known and most extreme exponent of the Neoclassical style in engraving, was a friend of Blake's, as was Henry Fuseli, who translated a work which helped to found the style: Winckelmann's *Reflections on the Painting and Sculpture of the Greeks* (1756; translation 1765).

Winckelmann asserted that Nature

> never could bestow the precision of Contour, that characteristic distinction of the ancients.
>
> The noblest Contour unites or circumscribes every part of the most perfect Nature, and the ideal beauties of the Greeks; or rather, contains them both.[12]

The Platonic tone of this is worth noting in view of Blake's alleged neo-Platonism. For the neo-Platonists, 'Spirit' or 'Intellect' or the 'Intelligible World' consisted of distinct, bounded Forms or 'Ideas'. Thomas Taylor, whose work Blake had probably read, refers to 'those regions of mind, where all things are *bounded* in intellectual measure; where every thing is permanent and beautiful, eternal and divine' (emphasis added).[13] These bounds or forms impose themselves on matter, giving it shape, and creating the world we see around us. But in the Intelligible World there is no such division between the Forms and Matter: there is no matter to impose on – the forms are, so to speak, the forms of themselves, and not an imposition on a recalcitrant substance. Furthermore, 'intellectual' bounds in themselves exist in a mode of infinity, and are not limited by Time and Space.

This paradoxical co-existence of the bounded and the infinite arises from what R.T. Wallis aptly calls the problem 'of reconciling the mystical desire to transcend form and limit with the Classical Greek view of them as the essence of perfection'.[14] And he goes on to point out that where Plotinus, who may be regarded as the most important neo-Platonist, 'decisively breaks with traditional Greek ideas is in regarding the very fact that Intelligence has limits as disqualifying its claim to be the highest reality'.[15] It is the unknowable *One* or *Good* that constitutes this reality for Plotinus, and one can only speak of it by saying what it is *not*, for words mislead:

> Indeed it is no one of the natures of which it is the principle; and it is such that nothing can be predicated of its nature, neither being, nor essence, nor life; for it is incomprehensibly raised above these. But if by taking away being you are able to apprehend this ineffable nature, you will immediately be filled with astonishment, and directing yourself towards him, and pursuing his latent retreats till you repose in his solitary deity, you will now behold him by a vision perfectly simple and one . . .

The One, 'though immense, is not measured by any magnitutude, nor limited by any circumscribing figure, but is every where immeasurable, as being greater than every measure, and more excellent than every quantity'.[16]

But this idea of an unknowable One has no place in Blake's philosophy. Such a notion was inimical to him: 'Think of a white cloud. as being holy you cannot love it but think of a holy man within the cloud love springs up in your thought. for to think of holiness distinct from man is impossible to the affections' (Annotations to Swedenborg's *Divine Love and Wisdom*, E603/K90). Because imagination is Blake's firm point of departure there is no room for abstraction and no room for an invisible, unknowable God.

Put together, his statements show that he thinks that the 'Infinite' and the 'bounded' are compatible: that the 'Infinite' contains bounded forms, and that these are perceived by the visionary. On the neo-Platonic principles, 'boundedness' and 'Infinity' were, in the last analysis, incompatible: this is what necessitated the distinction between the One and the Intelligible World. But for Blake the situation is perhaps best described in terms of his attitude to two concepts: on the one side you have the One, for Plotinus the source of all Forms; on the other, the material world. This dualism is precisely what Blake rejected. For him, the two have to go together. It is wrong to imagine that there is a separate 'spirit world' above, and equally wrong to think that there is an objective material world separate from our imaginations. Pater puts the aesthetic implications of such a position quite well in his essay on Winckelmann in *The Renaissance*: 'The mind begins and ends with the finite image, yet loses no part of the spiritual motive. That motive is not loosely or lightly attached to the sensuous form . . . but saturates and is identical with it.'[17] It is worth pondering this position: it implies not only that there is no 'objective reality', but also, what is perhaps more difficult to grasp, that there is no general or abstract meaning outside and beyond the world of appearances. Blake delights in the energy and 'boundlessness' of this world. He is against all reductions of this infinity to some principle of 'oneness' or identity. In accordance with these convictions, he revises neo-Platonism.

But that revision is very much part of contemporary history, not some arbitrary juggling of abstruse terms. Consider Plotinus's One for a moment: 'Indeed it is no one of the natures of which it is the principle.' Here we have the distinction between the world of differing forms on the one hand, and the principle of those forms, hidden beyond appearances, on the other. One may compare this to Voltaire's remarks on the rational deity, where he speaks, as we have seen, of the 'trifling difference between the vestments that cover our weak bodies, between our defective languages, our ridiculous customs, our numerous imperfect laws, our idle opinions, our several conditions, so disproportionate in our eyes, so equal in thine'. Here one has the same distinction between a unifying principle and its differing expressions, conceived as a kind of deceptive clothing or covering. One could rephrase Plotinus in terms of Voltaire: 'Indeed, the Reason is no one of the *vestments* of which it is the principle.' Blake delights, or wishes to delight, in the differing vestments of life. For him, the world of appearances is the only real world, as long as it is filled with imagination. But devoid of imagination, and considered as an objective material world, it becomes, indeed, a world of deceptive appearances.

Blake's revision of neo-Platonic terms, like his poetry in general, arises out of the problematic encounter of radical Christianity with Enlightenment discourses. He didn't just pick up some old neo-Platonic books and become a neo-Platonist. Rather, neo-Platonism became part of his battle against Enlightenment reductionism. This shying-away from unity, and courting of process, has its corollary in his poetry. Even from the *Songs* it must be clear that his work represents a sharp reversal of that process whereby, as Julia Kristeva says, 'The form of the relation (between unity and process) consists in the privileging of the unifying instance (the instance which established the coherence of the sign, and of the system and of sociality) at the expense of the process, which then becomes relegated to the sidelines under the heading of madness, holiness or poetry.'[18]

V

So far we have seen that in Blake there is a 'bad' *bound* and a 'good' *bound*. The 'bad' bound contains anything considered to be eternally fixed and definite, in particular the Newtonian universe and the world of experience as conceived by empiricism (the philosophy of the five senses); also that world as reproduced in imitative art, as, for instance, in strongly representational painting. The 'good' bound is the energetic and imaginative form given to things by the creative mind, or it is the energetic and individual form taken by things, without reference to a particular mind.

But the similarity in the terminology used for both conceptions shows that in fact they are closely allied. The Bard (who produces the 'good' bound) is always in danger of degenerating into the Priest or Druid (who guards the Holy Word of Scripture – which is in fact congealed poetry). This danger must provoke anxiety in the artist, and is one of the chief subjects of Blake's work. It motivates, for instance, the ambiguity of the 'Introduction' to *Experience*. And it is an important part of the subject of *Europe: A Prophecy* (1794). This is particularly obvious from the frequency with which the ideas of binding and bounds occur in that poem, and also in its concentration on the philosophy of the five senses. For this reason we shall depart from strict chronology and make *Europe* our point of departure among the longer poems. In fact the departure from chronology is not as wide as it might look. From at least 1791 Blake had been attempting to write long poems which would reflect on and explain the momentous political events of his time. In that year Joseph Johnson, the radical bookseller, printed the first book of Blake's *The French Revolution. A Poem in Seven Books*. It was never published, though, nor have the other six books ever been discovered. But it shows Blake giving an allegorical cast to historical events and personages. Thus the Archbishop of Paris is said to rise the address the French king and nobility 'In the rushing of scales and hissing of flames and rolling of sulphurous smoke' (1.127, E291/K140), a line which makes it clear that Blake regards the representatives of the *ancien régime* as devilish. There is, indeed, an air of the Parliament of fallen devils in Book II of *Paradise Lost*.

Blake then began work on a long poem about the American Revolution which for the first time makes use of many of the characters which were to remain as part of his developed mythology: Urizen, Los, Enitharmon and Orc. This poem ended up as *America* (1793) and, as I have shown elsewhere, as the text of parts of *Europe* (1794); the parts in question being those passages in plates 9, 10 and 12 written in a relatively regular loose heptameter (seven-stressed lines).[19] These lines concern 'Albions Angel', the spirit of reaction in England, and his fellow Angels, who hold a council which is also to some extent modelled on *Paradise Lost*, II.

It seems likely, then, that *Europe* dates from the period when *Songs of Experience* were being completed. Blake went on to write poems called *Africa* and *Asia*, which formed the two parts of *The Song of Los* (1795). He wished to show the history of mankind through a history of the four continents.

Without going into too much detail one may guess that the textual history of *Europe* is even more complex than the preceding remarks would indicate: it looks as if there are several different layers representing different times of composition. It is interesting, and it's a fact worth returning to, that Blake is probably the greatest reviser and cobbler-together of fragments and odd ends until T.S. Eliot. In any case, whatever the date of each piece, which is probably unknowable, the poem seems to fall fairly easily into five parts. These parts fit inside each other, so that one has a poem, within a poem, within a poem. The first part, present in only two of the twelve known copies of *Europe*, is a brief preface in which a fairy discourses with Blake about the limitations of the five senses, and then is said to begin dictating *Europe* to him. The second part, called the 'Preludium', describes how the 'nameless shadowy female', who represents this material world, complains to Enitharmon, the Eternal Female, about her own exhausting fertility. She has been impregnated by Orc, the spirit of revolution and representative of energy, and she is now bringing forth 'howling terrors, all devouring fiery kings' (2:4). She protests against Enitharmon's habit of giving 'solid form' to 'this vig'rous progeny of fires' (2:8).

The prophecy proper begins with the birth of Christ, and then documents the origins of Enitharmon's lust for dominion over man, which she achieves by spreading the doctrine that 'Womans love is Sin' (6:5). She controls men by inducing guilt about sex, and either withholding it, or seeming to give reluctantly. Elsewhere Blake calls Enitharmon's triumph an example of the 'Female Will', which he abhors. He associates the error with the Christian epoch, up until his own time, and would see an obvious institutional expression of it in the cult of the Virgin.

Part four of the poem is Enitharmon's dream, 'Eighteen hundred years' in duration (9:5). That is to say, her dream lasts the whole of the period from the birth of Christ up to Blake's own time. Her wishful dream becomes the reality of Europe, until Orc, the spirit of revolution, threatens to destroy the whole system. In the end the last trumphet is blown by 'A mighty Spirit . . . from the land of Albion / Nam'd Newton'. This indicates that, by distilling the philosophy of error into a particularly potent form, Newton has paradoxically strengthened the opposing forces which, in the end, will destroy that philosophy.

The fifth part of the poem begins with Enitharmon's waking from her dream (13:9). She calls to her sons and daughters, but they are rejoicing at the approaching dawn of revolution, which now begins in France.

Where does 'binding' and 'the bound' come into this? First in the frontispiece, where Urizen wields his compasses, leaning out over the abyss of the universe, binding and measuring the deep. The poem itself purports to show how this fixer and freezer of energies has been able to pose as God, with the help of Enitharmon. In the prefatory lines, where 'Blake' discourses with a fairy, the idea of the 'bounded' is associated, as so often, with the restricting Philosophy of the Five Senses:

> Five windows light the cavern'd Man; thro' one he
>   breathes the air;
> Thro' one, hears music of the spheres; thro' one, the
>   eternal vine

Flourishes, that he may recieve the grapes; thro' one
can look,

And see small portions of the eternal world that ever
groweth;

Thro' one, himself pass out what time he please, but
he will not;

For stolen joys are sweet, & bread eaten in secret
pleasant.

(iii:1–6, E60/K237)

It's notable that, though the five windows are limiting (one
only sees 'small portions' of the infinite through the eyes,
and 'Man' is said to be 'cavern'd') they are also liberating,
for they allow the perception of such beauty as Man can
perceive. And, indeed, their perceptions are described in
very positive terms: 'Thro' one, hears music of the spheres;
thro' one, the eternal vine / Flourishes, that he may receive
the grapes'. The sense of touch, which Blake compounded
with sexuality, for the sense of touch is distributed all over
the body, will permit humanity to escape from its imprison-
ment. But 'he will not; / For stolen joys are sweet, & bread
eaten in secret pleasant'. Although the tone is meant to be
disapproving, the force of the statement remains. Humanity
appears to be attracted by 'bound' sexuality, rather than by
the freedom which, according to Blake, would bring about
a change in human nature.

It is too easy to assume that Blake was an uncomplicated
exponent of free love. In fact there is much in his work to
suggest that not only did he see the existence of powerful
drives towards possessiveness and the desire to dominate,
but also he thought they were somehow constitutive of
human sexuality. This implied a limitation on the freedom
both of those dominated and of those who did the
dominating. But it also involved him in yet another
characteristic ambivalence about form: in this case the form
taken by human sexuality. Could it be that what was
delightful about human love was intimately bound up with
what was exclusive and potentially destructive in it? Blake
must have had a strong suspicion that this was so, for in a

poem from the Pickering Manuscript (*c.*1803) he was to picture himself as 'William Bond', bound by the ties of betrothal to 'Mary', tempted by other women, and particularly by the passion of one woman, for whom he threatens to leave Mary:

> For thou art Melancholy Pale
> And on thy Head is the cold Moons shine
> But she is ruddy & bright as day
> And the sun beams dazzle from her eyne
>
> (E497/K435)

Mary collapses, and 'William Bond' takes pity on her, deciding that in tenderness and sympathy, rather than in passion, are to be found the more enduring and essential aspects of love:

> I thought Love livd in the hot sun shine
> But O he lives in the Moony light
> I thought to find love in the heat of day
> But sweet Love is the Comforter of Night
>
> Seek Love in the Pity of others Woe
> In the gentle relief of anothers care
> In the darkness of night & the winters snow
> In the naked & outcast Seek Love there
>
> (E497–8/K436)

Whether or not these sentiments are true (and who can say?) there is at least the ghost of regret conveyed by the warm description of Mary's rival and by the name 'Bond', suggesting that William has settled for something less than he might have had, and feels constrained. If 'pity divides the soul / And man, unmans' (*Milton*, 8:19–20) William's may indeed be seen as a divided soul. And yet the poem poignantly expresses the way in which pity and tenderness may seem validly to override desire, in that the latter can exist without real knowledge of and sympathy for its object. Another ambivalence, then. But it is important for our argument to stress that this is an ambivalence about the way the 'bonds' of love operate.

It is an ambivalence which is relevant to some lines about 'binding' which occur in the 'Preludium' to *Europe*. The 'shadowy female' objects to her progeny being given 'solid form' by Enitharmon. Here 'form' is limiting, for the question is:

> And who shall bind the infinite with an eternal band?
> To compass it with swaddling bands? and who shall cherish it
> With milk and honey?
>
> (2:13–15, E61/K239)

Tenderness may be a way of belittling and attempting to bind the unpredictable energies which partake of infinity. In the 'Prophecy' Los delights in narrow bounds:

> The shrill winds wake!
> Till all the sons of Urizen look out and envy Los:
> Sieze all the spirits of life and bind
> Their warbling joys to our loud strings
> Bind all the nourishing sweets of earth
> To give us bliss, that we may drink the sparkling wine
> of Los
> And let us laugh at war . . .
>
> (4:1–7, E62/K239)

Now Los is the Eternal Poet, the Spirit of Prophecy. What he describes may seem like the mere description of the process of making song. But it does have a sinister air to it: the strings of the bardic harp become chains of bondage. This impression of something sinister is underlined by the air of rapacious enjoyment associated with the binding: 'Sieze all the spirits of life . . . To give us bliss . . .' Thus fortified, Los and his children will 'laugh at war'. And one of the purposes of this musical event is to arouse 'envy' in Urizen: hardly a pure artistic impulse. In fact this passage displays exactly the same ambivalence about poetic form as we found in the 'Introduction' to *Experience*. Indeed, Los is the Bard of *Experience* in mythological guise. Both the 'Introduction' and this passage from *Europe* takes the ambivalent view of the form as their subject: it is no mere sideline. This ambivalence rests on a fact about artistic form noted by Jacques Derrida: 'No doubt that by orienting and organizing the coherence of the system, the center of the structure permits the freeplay of its elements inside the total form. And even today the notion of a structure lacking any center represents the unthinkable itself. Nevertheless, the center also closes off the freeplay it opens up and makes possible.'[20] The structure is what makes freedom possible, but it is also what limits and even threatens it. Furthermore, since structure is what one artist inherits from another, as artistic 'convention', it threatens the freedom of future artists. For, if they slavishly follow convention, they will lose artistic energy and individuality, as Blake would see it: this is influence killing its own children. And yet structure is indispensable.

Derrida's description of structure *versus* freeplay has its roots in Romantic tradition, so its aptness to Blake is hardly surprising. But, where he is concerned to describe an oscillation that is endemic to all art, Blake wishes to show how artists may avoid the limiting-effects of structure. This is one of a number of related libertarian themes of *The Marriage of Heaven and Hell*. But even in that strident and apparently confident book one may detect many doubts about the extent to which it is possible to avoid the limits of structure and influence.

5 The Marriage of Heaven and Hell (c.1791–3)

I

We have seen that, while gesturing towards a perspective beyond those of the 'contraries' of *Innocence* and *Experience*, Blake doesn't actually provide one. To this extent he is faithful to the idea, expressed in *The Marriage of Heaven and Hell*, that outside contraries there is no stable point from which an objective perception can be achieved. Indeed, to imagine that there is such a point would only be to align oneself with one of the contraries: that of the Devourer, imagining oneself to possess the truth of 'Analytics', but in fact dependent on one's Prolific opposite.

In the *Songs* each perspective is shown to be both partial and powerful: powerful, indeed, by virtue of the very fact that it is expressed through limitations which alone can afford strength. For, without the limitations provided by a firm outline, a definite form, there is only weakness and indeterminacy. But we must not imagine that the 'contraries' of *Innocence* and *Experience* are necessarily congruent with the 'contraries' discussed in *The Marriage* just because Blake uses the same word and makes a statement that contraries always exist. Both *Innocence* and *Experience* show a troubled sense of entrapment, as well as of what lies outside the trap. Neither perspective is privileged over the other. But in *The Marriage* contraries are unlike the example of Innocence and Experience in that Blake wishes it to be understood that he firmly espouses one of his contraries, and firmly rejects the other. He is for Hell and against Heaven. He is for Evil, as commonly understood, and against Good. He is for Energy and against Reason, for the Prolific and against the Devourer. It will be seen that, unlike with Innocence and Experience, the contraries discussed in *The Marriage* conform to a general pattern whereby one polarity expresses Energy, or a kindred idea, and the other the lack of it. A couple of questions therefore occur: if the role of one of the polarities is merely to be the privation of the other, while at the same time being its pale reflection, in what sense can this 'weak' contrary be called a 'contrary' at all? Secondly, there is the question we raised at the beginning of the book: if the contraries really are complementary and necessary to each other, surely there must be some qualification to Blake's firm espousal of one rather than the other? For, while espousing one, he must always have been aware of the eternal necessity of the other. In line with this, the Songs of Innocence and of Experience are all qualification. But in *The Marriage,* apart from the bare admission of the necessity of contraries, Blake is ostensibly of the Devil's party, and rejects the opposing point of view, even though he admits its necessity.

The two questions have one longish answer: Blake is committed, for political reasons, to the espousal of revolutionary and libertarian Energy, and to the thesis that religions and codes of law derive from the energy of Poetic Genius. If his writings are to be politically effective, he must adopt the position he favours without equivocation. And according to his general thesis the 'other side', representing Reason, is completely dependent on Energy: it is the 'bound or outward circumference of Energy' (*MHH*, pl.4): it is a dead structure or shell, created by life, but from which the life has departed.

But not all contraries can be conceived in quite the same way. Blake mentions 'Love and Hate' (*MHH*, pl.3) for instance. Is Hate merely a pale reflection of love? Hardly, for Love and Hate really do seem to be contraries, in the sense that each has real and substantial power, unlike the Devourer in the Devourer/Prolific couple, which is merely parasitic on its opposite. The mention of 'Love and Hate' thus calls Blake's whole conception in *The Marriage* into question.

Innocence and Experience, on the face of it, represent yet another case: neither contraries in the sense of Love and Hate, nor an asymmetrical opposition where one term is subordinate to the other, as with Prolific and Devourer: Innocence and Experience seem, on the face of it, to represent two *successive* states of the human soul. In trying, with difficulty, to depict them as contraries, Blake reveals his anxiety about the possibility of achieving an original, untainted innocence.

So the word 'contrary' is by no means without its problems. As we remarked, the particular definition implied in *The Marriage* (Energy and its 'Negation', to use a later Blakean word) derives from Blake's desire to make an effective political intervention in the revolutionary period 1790–3. But he still reveals anxiety about the possible limitations of his point of view. This anxiety takes the form of an insecure over-assertiveness, an hysterical avowal. Blake protests too much. It is interesting to examine the formal effects of this insecurity in some detail.

II

Blake would have it that the voice that speaks in *The Marriage* is that of 'honest indignation', which is also 'the voice of God' and the voice of prophecy, since Isaiah says that this is the voice that moves in him (pl.12). At the very beginning of *The Marriage*, in 'The Argument', Blake explains how 'the just man' (Rintrah) came to adopt these indignant tones:

The Argument

Rintrah roars & shakes his fires in the burdend air;
Hungry clouds swag on the deep

Once meek, and in a perilous path,
The just man kept his course along
The vale of death.
Roses are planted where thorns grow.
And on the barren heath
Sing the honey bees.

Then the perilous path was planted:
And a river, and a spring
On every cliff and tomb;
And on the bleached bones
Red clay brought forth.

Till the villain left the paths of ease,
To walk in perilous paths, and drive
The just man into barren climes.

Now the sneaking serpent walks
In mild humility.
And the just man rages in the wilds
Where lions roam.

Ritnrah roars & shakes his fires in the burdend air;
Hungry clouds swag on the deep.

(E33/K148–9)

The import of this difficult little allegory is that the just
man once walked, courting danger by attempting to
influence those who lived without love, justice or art. His
manner was mild, and gradually the wilderness was made
fruitful and pleasant. This attracted the 'villain', who had
never wished to expend creative energy in the first place,
away from the 'paths of ease' (complete absence of effort or
energy) into the 'perilous paths', which have now been
made easy by the energy and artifice of the just man. The
'villain' is then able to inhabit the 'outlines' of a pleasant

and fruitful society. These outlines were created by the energy of the just man. The villain merely relaxes in them, and treats them as easy, given forms. This is the same idea as that which is conveyed on plate 16:

> The Giants who formed this world into its sensual existence and now seem to live in it in chains; are in truth. the causes of its life & the sources of all activity, but the chains are, the cunning of weak and tame minds. which have power to resist energy. according to the proverb, the weak in courage is strong in cunning.
>
> Thus, one portion of being, is the Prolific, the other, the Devouring (E40/K155)

But to return to 'The Argument': after the villain has left the 'paths of ease' to devour the 'products' the just man has created in the perilous paths, the just man leaves in disgust and goes off into the 'wilds' – not, this time, to exercise a mild influence, but to rage 'Where lions roam'.

The just man has, thus, seen the need for 'opposition' ('Opposition is true Friendship' – pl. 20, E42/K157). He has perceived 'contraries'. It is not sufficient always to give, out of the bounty of the Prolific, labour and imagination, only to find that one's products are devoured with no sense of the energy that went into them. To acquiesce in the notion that the world is a static, objective entity, which we passively consume, is to threaten the continuance of Imagination. The just man must therefore not merely create new worlds, new ideas, new artifacts; he must angrily insist on the fact that the world is indeed a product of human labour and imagination.

One interesting feature of this little allegory is the double displacement which occurs: the villain moves from the 'paths of ease' into the refurbished perilous paths; the just man moves from being meek in the perilous paths to being angry in the wilds. In particular the just man's 'voice of honest indignation' is something he has to adopt: it was not originally his, perhaps is not his 'true nature'.

And there are many signs in *The Marriage* that the just
man's voice becomes hoarse with a willed opposition and
firmness of point of view. Perhaps a 'firm perswasion' can
remove mountains as Blake says (pl.12), but this remains
one of the more difficult feats of human will. Yet that is,
with good scriptural authority, the example Blake gives of
the results of a 'firm perswasion'. The question of 'firm
perswasion' arises because Blake asks Isaiah and Ezekiel
'how they dared so roundly to assert. that God spake to
them; and whether they did not think at the time, that they
would be misunderstood, & so be the cause of imposition'.
We can take 'imposition' here to mean a strong, partial
interpretation. Isaiah supports 'firm perswasion' and thus
'imposition'. Blake agrees, for when the 'Angel' complains
that 'thy phantasy has imposed upon me', 'Blake' answers
'we impose on one another' (pl.20, E42/K157) And the
Proverb of Hell 'He who has sufferd you to impose on him
knows you' equates individual human identity with imposition – that is, with a particular point of view. All discourse
is governed by partial and limited interpretation, although,
as we have seen, this fact has its dangers. The ambivalent
view of imposition, which corresponds to that of 'bound', is
suggested by a couple of flourishes in Blake's illuminated
text. In the phrase 'cause of imposition' there is a small,
downward-descending bird, neatly placed above the word
'cause', and a kind of bracket, of the same size and similar
shape neatly placed below it. The effect is, indeed, that of a
frame or a pair of brackets, while ambivalence is suggested
by the bird: is its flying downwards, rather than upwards, a
bad sign? Or is it a symbol of inspiration because it is a
bird? Is this happy or unhappy imposition? After the word
'imposition' there is a vigorous, serpentine flourish which
could, by virtue of its vigour, suggest energy. Or, since
snakes often have an ambivalent meaning in Blake, it could
suggest the narrowing of energy into a crawling, snake-like
form.

Blake would have us believe that he is happy to impose:

> This Angel, who is now become a Devil, is my
> particular friend: we often read the Bible together in
> its infernal or diabolical sense which the world shall
> have if they behave well
>   I have also: The Bible of Hell: which the
> world shall have whether they will or no. (pl. 24, E44/
> K158)

The world shall have the Bible in its 'infernal' sense 'if they
behave well' – that is, if they are of a like mind with Blake,
and can read it in his way. But being of a like mind with
Blake is here jocularly conceived as 'behaving well', which
certainly suggests a willingness to impose, though the air of
ragging detracts from the seriousness of the impression, and
makes us wonder how certain Blake is about the efficacy of
'imposition'.

The Bible is an ambiguous document. Blake will also
offer the world an unambiguous Bible after the manner of
The Marriage of Heaven and Hell: 'The Bible of Hell'. The
world shall have it 'whether they will or no': there is
certainly 'imposition' here, and the desire to flaunt it,
though oddly undercut by 'I have also: The Bible of Hell' –
undoubtedly jocular, and sounding like something out of a
humble bookseller's catalogue. Again, insecurity. It is just
such insecure provocativeness that informs the brilliant
Proverbs of Hell, and the elements of a parody of
Swedenborg to be found throughout *The Marriage*.

III

The elements of a parody of Swedenborg. But only the
elements. It is often claimed that *The Marriage of Heaven and
Hell* is a full-blooded parody of the works of Emmanuel
Swedenborg, a visionary and mystic in the tradition of
Boehme and philosophical alchemy.[1] This claim cannot
bear much scrutiny. For, while it is true that Swedenborg's

works are attacked within the discourse of *The Marriage*, this discourse bears very little resemblance to Swedenborg's. 'The Prophets Isaiah and Ezekiel dined with me, and I asked them how they dared so roundly to assert. that God spake to them . . . ' Compare this dramatic directness with almost anything in Swedenborg:

> *INASMUCH* as there are infinite varieties in heaven, and no one society, nor indeed any one angel, exactly like another . . . therefore heaven is to be considered under the threefold distinction of general, special, and particular: in general, into two kingdoms; specifically, into three heavens; and in particular, into innumerable societies . . .[2]

These charactericially hair-splitting generalities are quite unlike the style of Blake's *Marriage*, which owes much to radical, popular Protestant prophesying. It is reminiscent, for instance, of a work by that pseudo-Bunyan George Larkin, which was long thought to be by Bunyan himself. In *Visions of John Bunyan . . . The Glories of Heaven, The Terrors of Hell*, the protagonist has a conversation with an Angel and with Elijah, and Elijah discourses on the risen body.[3]

But of course there are improtant references to Swedenborg in the text. And there is a repeated direct parody of chapter headings in Swedenborg: Blake writes 'A Memorable Fancy' for Swedenborg's 'A Memorable Relation', thus emphasizing his visionary powers, as opposed to the latter's literal-mindedness (as for instance in Swedenborg's assertion that 'Divine Influx' passes from God to Man 'through the forehead'[4]). By providing chapter headings, Swedenborg's work acts in the most concrete way as an 'outline' or 'bound' for Blake's – a weak outline, a Devourer's bound, against which a radical, oppositional discourse presses exuberantly and contemptuously. For Swedenborg lacks a 'firm perswasion' and evidences all the 'weakness of the plagiary', 'analysing' the ideas of other more creative writers; receiving them as the Devourer receives the 'excess' of the Prolific:

Now hear a plain fact: Swedenborg has not written one new truth: Now hear another: he has written all the old falshoods.

And now hear the reason. He conversed with Angels who are all religious, & conversed not with Devils who all hate religion, for he was incapable thro' his conceited notions.

Thus Swedenborgs writings are a recapitulation of all superficial opinions, and an analysis of the more sublime, but no further.

Have now another plain fact: Any man of mechanical talents may from ·the writings of Paracelsus or Jacob Behmen, produce ten thousand volumes of equal value with Swedenborg's. and from those of Dante or Shakespear, an infinite number.

But when he has done this, let him not say that he knows better than his master, for he only holds a candle in sunshine (pl.22, E43/K157–8).

That Swedenborg is a Devourer is the meaning of the passage at the beginning of *The Marriage* proper: 'As a new heaven is begun, and it is now thirty-three years since its advent: the Eternal Hell revives. And lo! Swedenborg is the Angel sitting at the tomb; his writings are the linen clothes folded up' (pl.3, E34/K149). Swedenborg is external form from which the life has departed: he is the Angel outside Christ's empty tomb, his writings the empty shroud. So it is only just that his writings should provide the mere chapter headings of Blake's *Marriage*. Furthermore, the purveyor of dead form is a plagiarist: he reproduces the opinions and devices of others in a lifeless manner.

And yet these lines give Swedenborg a certain importance. For without his 'outline' Blake's own text could not exist. The motifs from Swedenborg, and the references to him, thus stand in the same relationship to Blake's more properly characteristic prophesying-style as does the latter's idea of 'bound' or 'outline' to his idea of form: that of a framework (or frame) both indispensable and potentially vitiated by virtue of being a limit. In this case the outline provided by Swedenborg is signalled as vicious. But given the fact that Blake is to some extent parasitic on Swedenborg it's possible to see anxiety in his dismissal of the latter's claims to originality. Is Blake afraid that he himself is a plagiarist?

It would be wrong, however, to see *The Marriage* as a clash between one style that is parodied and another with which Blake feels happily identified. It's true that he is in the tradition of radical Protestantism, and true that in *The Marriage* we are directed to regard Blake's visions as the result of 'firm perswasion'. Yet these visions have a peculiar context: they have overtones of popular Protestant prophecy; but they appear within the unusual context of an illuminated book, and in juxtaposition with elements of a parody of Swedenborg. These facts make the visions of *The Marriage* themselves seem like a parody, or at least like a quotation: the clash of styles foregrounds style itself. Furthermore, popular prophecy was usually an imitation of the Bible, and Blake's work is no exception. As so often, he dissolves the boundary between parody and imitation. Or rather he shows that the boundary does not exist. For, if no literature can exist without precursors, all literature approaches the condition of parody. The difference between what is recognized as parody and what, by contrast, is deemed 'serious' or 'natural' is a matter of the degree to which the writer is successful in actually indicating 'misleading motivation' to the reader: 'Misleading motivation (the play upon generally known literary rules firmly entrenched in tradition and used by the author in other than their traditional ways) is indispensible for parody' (Boris Tomashevsky, 'Thematics').[5] Another part of the text will be indicated as 'natural', not parodic. But the mere fact of intertextuality decrees that parody be only a special way of inheriting influences.

Since neither the text parodied, nor the text which does the parodying, is the original expression of a unified author, no writer can escape irony. While wishing, perhaps, to assert the truth and completeness of a particular view, he or she is merely reproducing the limitations involved in specific modes of writing. This is true even when the author wishes to show that another author's text (for example, the object of parody) is limited. There is thus no danger of the unfortunate case considered by Roland Barthes: 'how can stupidity be pinned down without declaring oneself intelligent? How can one code be superior to another without abusively closing off the plurality of codes?'[6] Barthes provides what he takes to be an answer to his own questions: 'Only writing, by assuming the largest possible plural in its own taste, can oppose without appeal to force the imperialism of each language.'[7] But this answer must be qualified. For, while offensive attempts at foreclosure may be made, there is nevertheless no danger, precisely on Barthes's own terms, that a writer will succeed in closing off the text. On the other hand, one may pale at the vertiginous plurality suggested by Barthes. For this implies that, as Jonathan Culler says, 'What is set against appearance is not reality but the pure negativity of unarrested irony.'[8] Such an idea would not have appealed to Blake. His philosophy is more akin to that of Friedrich Schlegel, which permits the spirit no rest, whether in definite ideas or in irony about them: 'Es ist gleich tödlich für den Geist, ein System zu haben, und keins zu haben. Er wird sich also wohl entschliessen müssen, beides zu verbinden' (It is equally deadly for the spirit to have a system and to have none. It will thus have to decide to combine both); 'Man kann nur Philosoph werden, nicht es sein. Sobald man es zu sein glaubt, hört man auf es zu werden' (One can only become a philosopher, not be one. As soon as one believes that one is a philosopher, one ceases to become one).[9]

Anne Mellor comments on Schlegel's philosophy and on modern misunderstandings of it:

> Because for Schlegel both symbolism and allegory, both enthusiasm and irony are equally valid, the constant consciousness of the limits of human compre-

hension is not accompanied by despair, frustration, or existential *angst*. Most modern commentators have ignored the enthusiastic creativity inherent in Schlegel's concept of romantic irony. Perhaps they have been overly influenced by Hegel's description of irony as 'infinite absolute negativity' . . . In any case, they have assumed that romantic irony, or what Wayne Booth calls 'Unstable – Overt – Infinite Irony', leads only to an absurdist vision of a world where, as in the works of Samuel Beckett, 'all is chaos, when there is no point in living, when there is, in fact, no point in writing either' . . . But for Schlegel, as for Byron, Keats, and Carlyle, the chaos of the universe was fertile rather than destructive, and an ironic awareness of the limits of human understanding only posed a more exciting challenge to the alert and enthusiastically creative mind: to participate ever more expansively in the abundance of creative becoming.[10]

Since life, for Schlegel, is boundless chaotic energy, while the human struggle for order is inescapable, one must constantly seek that order, but never feel that one has achieved it. It's in something akin to this spirit that in *Jerusalem* Blake writes, 'I must Create a System, or be enslav'd by another Mans' (10:20, E153/K629), and of 'Striving with Systems to deliver Individuals from those Systems' (11:5 E154/K630). The 'system' must be a creation of the individual. Inherited systems are deadly, for by virtue of being inherited they represent 'imposition' without energy – deadly 'bound or outward circumference'. This can be illustrated from a passage on plate 11 of *The Marriage* about the origins of religion in poetic mythologies:

The ancient Poets animated all sensible objects with Gods or Geniuses, calling them by the names and adorning them with the properties of woods, rivers, mountains, lakes, cities, nations, and whatever their enlarged & numerous senses could percieve.

And particularly they studied the genius of each city
and country. placing it under its mental deity.

Till a *system* was formed, which some took advantage
of & enslav'd the vulgar by attempting to realize or
abstract the mental dieties from their objects: thus
began Priesthood. (E38/K153; emphasis added)

Here 'system' takes its place alongside 'abstraction': it is
produced by taking 'portions of existence' and fancying
that they are 'the whole'. It is *imposed* on 'the vulgar'. But
when Los says, in *Jerusalem*, 'I must Create a System or be
enslav'd by another Mans', he means that he must be
'animating' like the 'ancient Poets', rather than 'enslav'd'
by the imposition of abstract, inherited forms. Of course,
strictly speaking there is no necessary connection between
inheritance (or indebtedness) and abstraction. But Blake
thinks there is: for him vision is supposed to be always
original and individual. By accepting 'another man's'
system one has ensured that, for oneself, that system is
dead.

But Blake's texts reveals an uneasy awareness that such a
notion is untenable. Their constant use of quotation,
parody and derived terms lays bare their indebtedness and
undermines the 'firm perswasion' of originality. Thus, in
The Marriage, anxiety about the possibility of exerting an
untainted, original 'firm perswasion' is inscribed in the
text's status as a clear imitation of popular Protestant
visionary writings, as much as in its assertiveness and in its
protesting too much that Swedenborg is totally derivative.
This anxiety expresses itself at the thematic level in an
insistence on the secondariness of the proponents of
'Reason'. For there are at least five parallel myths of
usurpation: that of the just man by the villain (pl.2); that of
Satan by Messiah (pls.5–6); that of 'ancient Poets' by
priests (pl.11); that of Giants or Prolifics by the 'weak' or
Devourers (pl.16); and that of the visionaries (Paracelsus,
Boehme, Dante, Shakespeare and Blake) by Swedenborg
(pls.21–2). *The Marriage of Heaven and Hell* is a counter-

usurpation intended to represent the proponents of Reason as mere outline or circumference, and in particular to humiliate Swedenborg by making him the outline for a text of which the 'Energy' consists in a grafting of popular vision onto notions of the Sublime.

The myth of usurpation is another way of conceiving the oscillation between form as expressive and form as limiting: the latter usurps the former. It is a myth which is fundamental to the longer poems.

6 Usurpation and Confusion of Powers

I

Blake's 'Prophetic Books' (not 'prophecies' in the colloquial sense: more like visionary analyses) clearly grow out of the historical context we described in Chapter 1. They attempt to imitate the Bible in their parallelisms and sublime rhetoric:

> Why cannot the Ear be closed to its own destruction?
> Or the glistning Eye to the position of a smile!
> Why are Eyelids stord with arrows ready drawn,
> Where a thousand fighting men in ambush lie?
> *(Book of Thel*, 6:11–14, E6/K130)

In this they align themselves both with popular prophecy and with the Romantic praise of the Bible's sublimity.

They conjure up a shadowy, vast, heroic world of characters such as 'Theotormon' and 'Oothoon'. This is probably intended to evoke Macpherson's *Ossian*, where there are such characters as 'Oithona'. Thus they would be attempts at 'primitive' epic poetry as contemporary readers imagined it to be. The home-made mythology was influenced by contemporary researches into the similarities between the myths of different countries, but also by the contemporary belief that myths originated in inspired poetry.

The loose seven-stress metre of most of the prophecies

(very loose in *Milton* and *Jerusalem*) is a kind of half-way house between the poetic prose of the Bible and *Ossian* on the one hand, and Homer's hexameters and Milton's pentameters on the other.

Stylistically, then, the books attempt to look and sound like the work of such primitive but inspired poet-prophets as people then believed to have existed. In this they are an implicit correction of Milton, who, to Blake's way of thinking, had not gone far enough in his love of freedom, metrical or otherwise. But Milton was still to be admired and emulated as the sublime prophet of Christian Liberty, who had attempted not only to justify the ways of God to men, but also to allegorize the ways of Parliament: for it would never have occurred to Blake, or indeed to many of his contemporaries, to doubt that *Paradise Lost* contained a measure of political allegory.[1] An obvious stratagem was to 'do a Milton', both by revealing the true nature of divinity (consisting of projections made by human beings) and by including allegories of his own revolutionary epoch in his mythology. For Blake, with his libertarian beliefs, it would seem like an attractive idea to make his own poems the vehicles of a myth which reversed the conventional values of God and Satan. But there were certain difficulties in practice.

II

In Blake's work as a whole the principle of Energy or Imagination (not always the same thing, however) is constantly in danger of being usurped by that of Reason, or dead 'system'. Or else there is a kind of oscillation between the two principles; or even, as in the 'Introduction' to *Experience*, uncertainty about whether the two do or do not shade into each other. This uncertainty is reflected in a curious similarity in the imagery used to describe the principle of revolutionary Energy on the one hand and the principle of reactionary Reason on the other. It comes down to the problem that Blake, being of the Devil's party, associates Energy with Satan. But, wishing to show that the adherents of 'Reason' are in fact evil, though they pretend to be 'Angels', he depicts them also in Satanic terms. The results can be confusing.

In *The French Revolution* the Archbishop of Paris is able to describe the God who presides over the 'fallen world' of tyranny and oppression.

> An aged form, white as snow, hov'ring in mist, weeping in the uncertain light,
> Dim the form almost faded, tears fell down the shady cheeks; at his feet many cloth'd
> In white robes, strewn in air censers and harps, silent they lay prostrated;
> Beneath, in the awful void, myriads descending and weeping thro' dismal winds,
> Endless the shady train shiv'ring descended, from the gloom where the aged form wept.
> At length, trembling, the vision sighing, in a low voice, like the voice of the grasshopper whisper'd:
> My groaning is heard in the abbeys, and God, so long worshipp'd, departs as a lamp
> Without oil; for a curse is heard hoarse thro' the land, from a godless race
> Descending to beasts; they look downward and labour and forget my holy law;
> The sound of prayer fails from lips of flesh, and the holy hymn from thicken'd tongues;
> For the bars of Chaos are burst; her millions prepare their fiery way
> Thro' the orbed abode of the holy dead, to root up and pull down and remove,
> And Nobles and Clergy shall fail from before me, and my cloud and vision be no more;
> The mitre become black, the crown vanish, and the scepter and ivory staff
> Of the ruler wither among bones of death; they shall consume from the thistly field,

And the sound of the bell, and voice of the sabbath,
    and singing of the holy choir,
Is turn'd into songs of the harlot in day, and cries of
    the virgin in night.
They shall drop at the plow and faint at the harrow,
    unredeem'd, unconfess'd, unpardon'd;
The priest rot in his surplice by the lawless lover, the
    holy beside the accursed,
The King, frowning in purple, beside the grey
    plowman, and their worms embrace together.
(11.131–50, E292/K140–1)

The decrepitude of the 'aged form' in the 'cloud and vision' echoes that of the King of France himself: we are told as much in the first lines of the poem:

The dead brood over Europe, the cloud and vision
    descends over chearful France;
O cloud well appointed! Sick, sick: the Prince on his
    couch, wreath'd in dim
And appalling mist . . .
(11.1–3, E286/K134)

These passages provide a striking example of Blake's symbolizing the idea that God the Father is a reflection of the fallen state of mind. It is interesting to compare them with the first version of *God Judging Adam* (pen and watercolour, *c*.1790–3, private collection, England).[2] In this (unlike in the 1795 colour print in the Tate) God and Adam are almost comically alike: each has long white hair and a voluminous long white beard. Unlike in the colour print, God's chariot is surrounded by grey clouds, which, as in *The French Revolution*, convey the idea of hazy or weakened vision, while at the same time representing the conception of an external deity above the clouds. The rebellious people in the Archbishop's monologue have no such conception: they seem to have acquired the belief that soul and body are one. To the 'aged form' this means that they are 'Descending to beasts' and he refers to their 'lips of flesh' and 'thicken'd tongues'. They are a 'godless race' and forget the 'holy law' of the aged form, like the 'lawless race' of Har. The absence of Law seems to the aged form like 'Chaos'. But Blake suggests that mankind is about to take on the organic form of a united soul and body: the 'bars of Chaos' are, to him, the doors of the infinite.

It should be noted that the Archbishop of Paris is described in terms of Satanic imagery:

> risen from beneath the Archbishop of Paris arose,
> In the rushing of scales and hissing of flames and rolling of sulphurous smoke.
>
> (11.126–7, E291/K139–40)

This is the first example we come across of Blake's ambiguous use of Satanic imagery. It can cause confusion. The problem is best stated quite crudely: in *The Marriage of Heaven and Hell* there is much that encourages the idea that Blake simply reversed the values of God and Satan: God bad, Satan good. One problem with this is, as David Wagenknecht points out, that there is no conclusive evidence that Orc was 'originally benign', though I should add the proviso 'if we ignore *The Marriage of Heaven and Hell*.'[3] But John Beer sees Blake's attitude to 'Milton's Satan' as implying criticism. I think, granted that there is ambivalence towards Orc in the early Lambeth books, that the tone of *The Marriage of Heaven and Hell* is overwhelmingly in favour of what Morton D. Paley calls 'the Sublime of Energy'.[4] Therefore the passage on *Paradise Lost* must be read in the light of this fact.

This is not to deny that Blake must have given intellectual assent to the idea that Energy was vitiated in the fallen world. But at the time of *The Marriage* he seems to have thought that Energy would ensure a necessary purging of a world dominated by Reason. Thus, if Blake's works of 1790–4 give grounds for conflicting interpretations of Orc and Milton's Satan, it may be because the problems were not focused in Blake's mind as yet. There is much to be said for the traditional view that disillusionment with the course of the French Revolution concentrated his mind in this regard.

As for *The Marriage*, if some critics have supposed that a reversal of values takes place there, that is surely because such a reversal does take place. The idea of a World Turned Upside Down would be quite familiar to a radical Protestant, as Graham Pechey points out.[5] People were still writing in these terms in the Eighteenth Century:

> If a poor man to the market goes
>   To buy a bushel of wheat,
> Money and hat must be in hand,
>   Submission to the great
> . . .
> Beelzebub, grand Prince of Hell,
>   To whom these slaves are bound,
> He'll call them home and scourge them well,
>   O the World's turn'd Upside-Down.[6]

But the case must rest on the text of *The Marriage*: 'Evil is the active springing from Energy . . . Energy is the only life and is from the Body . . . Energy is Eternal Delight' (pls.3–4, E34/K149).

Confusion may arise from this reversal of values because the positive Satanic figure of whom Blake approves (usually Orc) is likely to be associated with flames and the serpent. But the negative Satanic figures, the evil tyrants and hypocrites who pretend to be Angels, may also carry these associations, as in the case of the Archbishop of Paris; for this is an obvious way of unmasking the truth behind the appearance of sacred religious and political authority. Thus, in some Notebook poems written not long after *The French Revolution* the repressive role of Priesthood is associated with the Satanic serpent (in the worst sense):

> Why darkness & obscurity
> In all they words & laws
> That none dare eat the fruit but from
> The wily serpents jaws
>
> ('To Nobodaddy', E471/K171)

And at the beginning (*c*.1790) of *The Marriage* we learn that 'Now the sneaking serpent walks / In mild humility' (pl.2).

The whole question is complicated further by the unequivocally pejorative sense of the word 'Satan' in Blake's later work.

A very obvious use of the reversal we have been discussing is to turn *Paradise Lost* upside down. This is what Blake does. By 1790 he was already obsessed with Milton and seems to have been groping towards his own system by criticizing him. We have the evidence of the famous passage about 'Milton's Messiah' on plates 5 and 6 of *The Marriage* (E34/K149–50). But there is also the series of drawings in the Notebook which appears to be for *Paradise Lost*: some of them definitely are.[7] And there is the use of allusions to Milton in the early prophetic books, such as *The French Revolution*.

The passage from *The Marriage of Heaven and Hell*, though very well known, is worth bearing in mind here:

> Those who restrain desire, do so because theirs is weak enough to be restrained; and the restrainer or reason usurps its place & governs the unwilling.
>
> And being restraind it by degrees becomes passive till it is only the shadow of desire.
>
> The history of this is written in Paradise Lost. & the Governor or Reason is call'd Messiah.
>
> And the original Archangel or possessor of the command of the heavenly host, is calld the Devil or Satan and his children are call'd Sin & Death
>
> But in the Book of Job Miltons Messiah is call'd Satan.
>
> For this history has been adopted by both parties
>
> It indeed appear'd to Reason as if Desire was cast out. but the Devils account is, that the Messiah fell. & formed a heaven of what he stole from the Abyss
>
> This is shewn in the Gospel, where he prays to the Father to send the comforter or Desire that Reason may have Ideas to build on, the Jehovah of the Bible

being no other than he, who dwells in flaming fire.

Know that after Christs death, he became Jehovah.

But in Milton; the Father is Destiny, the Son, a Ratio of the five senses. & the Holy-ghost, Vacuum!

Note. The reason Milton wrote in fetters when he wrote of Angels & God, and at liberty when of Devils & Hell, is because he was a true Poet and of the Devils party without knowing it

As John Beer points out, the acuteness of this passage has often been praised, but usually for the remark that Milton was 'of the Devils party without knowing it'.[8] Helen Gardner is another exception to this rule: she says: '*contraria sunt aequalia*, and Satan and the Son seem balanced against each other, as Blake saw them to be [in *Paradise Lost*]'.[9] She also notes that, because Satan and Hell precede Christ and Heaven in *Paradise Lost*, the latter are likely to seem like a 'parody' of the former.[10] I would add that Blake has noticed that it is only after Satan has fallen that Christ is raised to the status of Messiah. The Messiah, then, may seem to have replaced Lucifer. And thus, given Blake's reversal of values, Messiah will look like an usurper. The remark that 'in the Book of Job Miltons Messiah is call'd Satan' shows the precise nature of Blake's objection to Milton's Christ. For the Job Satan is concerned to test righteousness, conceived of as adherence to a moral standard: 'Doth Job fear God for nothing? . . . Thou has blessed the work of his hands . . . But put forth thine hand now, and touch all that he hath, and he will curse thee to thy face' (Job 1:9–11). The same would be true of Milton's Messiah from Blake's point of view:

> Happy for man, [grace] so coming; he her aid
> Can never seek, once dead in sins and lost;
> Atonement for himself or offering meet,
> Indebted and undone, hath none to bring.
> (*Paradise Lost*, III.232–5)

And in Book VI of *Paradise Lost* God refers to Messiah, who 'by right of merit reigns' and to the law of 'right reason'

(II.42–3). The Job Satan and 'Milton's Messiah' both adhere to a rationally apprehensible abstract moral standard – to the idea of Natural Law.

Messiah, 'the Governor or Reason' (so-called because of Swedenborg's description of 'the great Governor of heaven and hell'[11]) has usurped Lucifer's Titanic Energy. So much would be evident to Blake from the fact that Lucifer is indeed the original 'possessor of the command of the heavenly host' and the Son is only exalted, at a definite point in time, in Book III: as the Father says to Him,

> All power
> I give thee; reign for ever, and assume
> Thy merits; under thee as Head supreme
> Thrones, Princedoms, Powers, Dominions, I reduce.
> All knees to thee shall bow, of them that bide
> In heaven, or earth, or under earth in hell . . .
>
> (*Paradise Lost*, III.317–22)

And in Book V we hear of 'The great Messiah, and his *new* commands' (l.691; emphasis added).

Blake's sense of this usurpation is conveyed in the powerful sketch on pages 110 and 111 of the Notebook, where we see, as Erdman says, 'God the Father giving directions to the Son to save mankind from Satan, who hovers over the abyss or (as we take note of the web of lines around him) struggles like a trapped fly'.[12] The web of lines, which draws these figures into a unity, also indicates that God the Father, the Son and Satan are more closely related than Heaven might admit. It is worth noting the gloomy expression and rigid (almost tense) posture of the seated Father, clearly Urizenic; the meek and submissive attitude of the Son; and the muscular vigour of the naked Satan, who seems to be but recently fallen.

In fact the sketch might just as well serve as an illustration to the then-famous German poet Friedrich Klopstock's *Messiah*: Blake was thinking about Klopstock at this time.[13] Klopstock's Messiah says:

O my FATHER, I know that thou wilt reward my ready
submission to thy will, and that miriads of applauding
angels will witness and hail my triumph before the
eternal throne.

Thus spake JESUS, and arose. In his countenance
shone sublimity, filial love, and resignation.[14]

Klopstock was not, even unconsiously, of the Devil's party.
His work, Blake implies in the Notebook (page 1) gives
unequivocal aid and comfort to Nobodaddy.

Nobodaddy, a figure who never emerges from the
Notebook, is a clear precursor of Urizen. In 'To Nobodaddy'
he hides himself in clouds and he is dark and obscure; he is
the product not of clear vision but of abstract systematizing.
He is Nobody because 'abstraction of mental deities' has
created him. However, abstract systems are the basis for
the Law: hence Nobodaddy is also the 'Father of Jealousy'.
Jealousy causes war: Nobodaddy loves 'hanging & drawing
& quartering / Every bit as well as war & slaughtering'
(E499/K185). But he is also, in line with the ambiguous
Satanic imagery we have been discussing, the 'wily
serpent'. In this avatar he can be related to the 'sneaking
serpent' whose 'mild humility' is scorned in the 'Argument'
to *The Marriage*. The two aspects of Nobodaddy are also the
differing qualities of King and Priest – hanging and
quartering on the one hand, and sneaking humility on the
other. The connection of these two traits is much clearer
now, however: each has its roots in the jealous denial of
Energy. As far as *Paradise Lost* is concerned, Blake's sketch
of Father, Son and Satan in the Notebook suggests that he
associates the orthodox conception of Christ with hypocritical humility (sneaking serpent), and the Father with
tyranny. In his own myth-making, however, both traits are
subsumed under Nobodaddy, or Urizen.

Another example of the reversal of the values of *Paradise
Lost* can be found in those sections of *America* and *Europe*
which, like *The French Revolution*, contain elements of a
parody of *Paradise Lost*, II. The truth is that before he wrote

either *America* or *Europe* Blake was writing at least a fragment which would show the reaction of the English King and Parliament to the American Revolution much as *The French Revolution* had treated the French King and Parliament. This can be seen from a careful examination of the texts of *America* and *Europe*, and of the cancelled plates of *America*.[15]

What is particularly interesting is that some time from 1790 to 1793 Blake should be trying to write a poem, which alludes to Book II of *Paradise Lost*, in which each of the opposing figures is described in the same Satanic terms: Albion's Angel, the reactionary force, is 'The fiery King' and his temple is 'serpent-form'd' (*Europe*, 10:2, E62/K241) like Orc, who is 'a Human fire fierce glowing' (*America*, 4:8, E52/K197). Blake seems to have been disturbed by this similarity in what were supposed to be opposing forces. In cancelled plate *c* of *America* all phrases suggestive of fire and heat are deleted where they apply to Albion's Angel, and are replaced by phrases redolent of coldness (deleted phrases in square brackets):

> silent stood the King breathing [with flames] [hoar frosts] damp mists,
> And on his [shining] aged limbs they clasp'd the armour of terrible gold.
> Infinite London's awful spires cast a dreadful [gleam] cold . . .
> > (ll.5–7, K205 [from Keynes, for clarity's sake, but see E58])

Nevertheless, in the final version of *America*, Albion's Angel remains fiery. But in the original version there was an attempt to show that Albion's Angel was a venerable-seeming disguise, with 'snowy beard' and 'white garments' adopted by the real character 'Albions fiery Prince', who subsisted beneath the disguise.

This vacillation in Blake's use of symbolism reflects the fact that both Albion's Angel and Orc are subject to the laws of Urizen's universe: if the latter is constrained to the closed form of a serpent, the former is the instrument of that constraint.

III

If Energy and Reason may sometimes be unexpectedly described in the same terms, Imagination and Reason, equally unexpectedly, sometimes seem to act in similar ways. In the 'Preludium' to *America: A Prophecy* (1793), a poem which sees the American Revolution as the prelude to apocalypse, we first encounter that curious myth whereby Los (the spirit of poetry and prophecy) rivets his son Orc (the spirit of Energy and revolution) with 'tenfold chains' (1:12). In *The Book of Urizen* (1794) we learn that Los has chained Orc because he is jealous of the child's relationship with his mother, Enitharmon (20:9–24). The chain is called 'the Chain of Jealousy' (20:24). For, whereas Orc is relatively formless, but powerful, Energy, Los represents the creation of form, both artistic and political. He knows that he needs the Energy represented by Orc; or rather he both fears it, and needs to discipline it for the purposes of art. The binding of Orc is parallel to Los's binding of the 'spirits of life' for the purposes of artistic creation in *Europe* (pls. 3 and 4, discussed in Chapter 4 above). At one level this is an allegory of political institutions, which must both give shape to human energies (Orc) and at the same time avoid the repression and complete extinction of energy represented by Urizen. Los is torn between inchoate energy and moribund form. Clearly this is also an allegory about the artist.

Both Energy and Imagination, then, seem to share certain features with the Reason and 'system' into which they may degenerate: the vigorous serpent of Energy shades into the creeping serpent of Reason; the living form created by Los is dependent on the 'binding' of Energy. Everything fits with the picture of a writer made anxious by the possibility that even those forms that seem most liberating may easily degenerate into chains of slavery.

This anxiety is visible in a curiously subtle and unexpected way in a work of impassioned libertarian rhetoric, *Visions of the Daughters of Albion* (1793). The plot is by no means obscure. The virgin Oothoon wanders in the vale of Leutha, which in this poem represents Innocence on the verge of Experience, and plucks a 'Marygold', which represents her willingness to enter the world of sexual experience. She loves one Theotormon and makes her way towards his American domains, but the stern Bromion intercepts and rapes her. He then addresses Theotormon:

> behold this harlot here on Bromions bed,
> And let the jealous dolphins sport around the lovely
>   maid;
> Thy soft American plains are mine, and mine thy
>   north & south:
> Stampt with my signet are the swarthy children of the
>   sun:
> They are obedient, they resist not, they obey the
>   scourge:
> Their daughters worship terrors and obey the violent:
>
> Now thou maist marry Bromions harlot, and protect
>   the child
> Of Bromions rage . . .   (1:18–23, 2:1–2, E46/K190)

Bromion is a Puritan and, it seems probable, a slave-owner. (Blake had recently been illustrating a book by J.G. Stedman about the tortures inflicted on black slaves.) Bromion cannot conceive of permitting love without possession, and Oothoon's love for Theotormon thus seems to him to be defiled. But, since sexual passion seems fundamentally filthy to him in any case, he merely takes her freedom as an excuse for sating his lusts without love and respect: she has forfeited these gifts by not bearing the 'stamp' of any man.

Theotormon, the god-tormented one, is the idealistic Puritanical spirit of America. But his attitude to sexuality, particularly female sexuality, is hardly more enlightened than that of Bromion. For now he binds 'the adulterate pair' back to back in Bromion's caves (2:5) and sits lamenting Oothoon's supposed loss of purity. Oothoon blames Urizen, the 'Father of Jealousy' (7:12), for the possessiveness that afflicts even the idealistic and sensitive Theotormon, and that sullies his understanding of love. And in general her speech is a ringing call for diversity and freedom, against the Urizenic tendency to reduce everything to one identical principle, that of universally apprehensible justice and reason. As she says,

> Does the whale worship at thy footsteps as the hungry
>   dog?
> Or does he scent the mountain prey, because his
>   nostrils wide
> Draw in the ocean? does his eye discern the flying
>   cloud
> As the ravens eye? or does he measure the expanse like
>   the vulture?
> Does the still spider view the cliffs where eagles hide
>   their young?
>   (5:33–7, E49/K193)

It is entirely characteristic of Blake to link the sexual, the political and the religious in the manner of *Visions of the Daughters of Albion*, which is his first wide-ranging assault on patriarchal possessiveness – and indeed Urizen, the tyrannical but exhausted father god, appears for the first time here. But Blake is often more fortunate with his brilliant attacks on Urizen's bounded universe than he is with the description of the freedom he would put in its place. Leopold Damrosch comments acutely[16] on the curiously binding nature of the free love Oothoon recommends to Theotormon:

> But silken nets and traps of adamant will Oothon
>   spread,
> And catch for thee girls of mild silver, or of furious
>   gold
>   (7:23–4, E50/K194)

Another case of Blake depicting freedom in the guise of constraint; another clue to the difficulty he found in depicting freedom without some hint of bondage.

IV

If *Visions of the Daughters of Albion* represents an area of Experience, the earlier *Book of Thel* (1789, with additions *c*.1791) shows the limitations of Innocence becoming sinister.

Thel wanders in the vales of Har (limited Innocence). She is obsessed by her own mortality and transience. She encounters the 'Lilly of the valley', the Cloud, the Worm and the Clod of Clay. These represent the cycle of nature. She asks how she can delight in the world around her and in her own life, since she must die. They respond that she must cease to be obsessed with her own finiteness and transience and, in spiritual generosity and love, consider herself rather as part of the grand scheme of things. As the Cloud puts it,

> Then if thou art the food of worms. O virgin of the
> skies,
> How great thy use. how great thy blessing; every thing
> that lives,
> Lives not alone, nor for itself . . .
>
> (3:25–7, E5/K129)

On plate 6 Thel encounters her own grave-plot, and hears the voice of her own fears issuing from it:

> Why cannot the Ear be closed to its own destruction?
> Or the glistning Eye to the poison of a smile!
> Why are Eyelids stord with arrows ready drawn,
> Where a thousand fighting men in ambush lie?
> Or an Eye of gifts & graces, show'ring fruits & coined
> gold!
> Why a Tongue impress'd with honey from every
> wind?

> Why an Ear, a whirlpool fierce to draw creations in?
> Why a Nostril wide inhaling terror trembling &
>   affright.
> Why a tender curb upon the youthful burning boy!
> Why a little curtain of flesh on the bed of our desire?
> (6:11–20, E6/K130)

The infinite, in its sublimity, appears only terrifying to Thel. ('The roaring of lions, the howling of wolves, the raging of the stormy sea, and the destructive sword. are portions of eternity too great for the eye of man' *MHH*, pl.8.) It is hardly surprising that she is a victim of the Philosophy of the Five Senses, dividing the infinite into five different compartments. She might escape into infinity through the fifth sense (touch, or sexuality) but she is afraid to do so, and, as we learn, flees with a shriek back into the vales of Har (pls.21–2).

So far, so simple. But we might note that, whereas with Eye, Ear Tongue and Nostril she complains of the irrestrainable terrors of Experience, with sexuality she seems to be complaining precisely that it is restrained; the hymen, which is referred to in the last line, representing a barrier in the very place where desire is satisfied. This inconsistency reveals the intrusion of Blake's own obsessions, for he is never sure that Desire or Imagination can go unhindered by limits. With artistic form, for instance, he suffers from an anxiety similar to that which Maud Ellmann analyses in Pound, in an essay which draws heavily on Derrida's discussion of the hymen in 'The Double Session'.[17] Form, like the hymen, may seem both 'bearer' and 'barrier': 'progenitor and prophylactic, the hymen stands between desire and its perpetration, eternally both barren and prolific'.[18] What is expressed must be articulated in a substantial medium. This will never be the instantaneous expression of some unified thought, but will be manifold, and probably contradictory to a degree. In writers such as Blake and Pound, who desire the pure expression of original thoughts and perceptions, form, or even language itself, may seem irredeemably corrupt. And yet they are the means of creation, and the only ones available or possible. In Blake's anxious and ambivalent classification of barriers, the hymen takes its place alongside 'bound', 'veil', 'outline', 'circumference', 'garment' and, of course, Urizen's 'horizon'.

The Book of Urizen (1794)

I

'Of the primeval Priests assum'd power' is the first line of
the 'Preludium' to *The Book of Urizen* (1794). We are
immediately made aware that this is intended to be a book
about the original usurpation of Eternity by Reason, of
Imagination by Priesthood. We can easily associate Urizen
with the Angels' party of *The Marriage of Heaven and Hell*,
because he is said to be 'unprolific' (3:2), and therefore
presumably a Devourer of others' energies. And he is also
said to be 'abstracted' (3:6), and may thus be like those
originators of 'Priesthood', on plate 11 of *The Marriage*, who
'abstract the mental deities from their objects'.

These are indeed vital clues to the nature of Urizen, who
represents Blake's attempt to isolate the original cause and
condition of error. But *The Book of Urizen* is a much fuller
analysis of error than *The Marriage* and a much more
uncertain one.

It is important to note the peculiar and paradoxical
process by which Urizen's world is formed. For his chief
action, if that is the word, is to separate himself and
withdraw from the world of the 'Eternals', the name Blake
gives to the other shadowy godlike figures, who at this time
are supposed to exist in a paradisal state of creative energy
('Death was not, but eternal life sprung' – 3:39). He thus
becomes, in himself, like the 'bound or outward circum-

ference of Energy'. His error is to imagine that such an outline can be self-sufficient. For it should take the shape given to it by Energy, whereas Urizen, while withdrawing to the bounds of the universe, nevertheless wishes, at the same time, to impose these bounds as a limit.

The other thing that Urizen does is to form a 'vacuum' (3:5). His universe, and he himself, constitute a 'void' (3:4) because they lack the energy to be anything else. Indeed, perhaps the best way of picturing Urizen's world is as an empty shell: a vacuum within and a hard brittle shell without. In fact, Blake later comes to refer to the fallen world as the 'Mundane Shell', a term derived from neo-Platonic philosophy, but one to which he gives his own meaning, which includes the suggestion of something like Urizen's world as here described.

The very form of the poem is made to suit the moment when poetry congeals into scripture. The columns of verse, divided into chapters and numbered sections, are intended to look like a sacred scripture. More specifically, they are intended to look like a late eighteenth-century notion of the original poetic form of biblical prophecy. For people had come to realize that the Hebrew prophets had been poets perhaps not unlike the 'ancient Bards' of Albion. Robert Lowth's translation of the Bible had tried to convey the true nature of Hebrew 'sacred poetry'. Consider the beginning of his *Isaiah* (1791):

> 2 HEAR, O ye heavens; and give ear, O earth!
> For it is JEHOVAH that speaketh.
> I have nourished children, and brought them up;
> And even they have revolted from me.
> 3 The ox knoweth his possessor;
> And the ass the crib of his Lord:
> But Israel knoweth not Me;
> Neither doth my people consider.[1]

This is the kind of resuscitation of Hebrew sacred poetry that Blake is imitating, both in rhythm and in arrangement on the page:

4 From the depths of dark solitude. From
The eternal abode in my holiness,
Hidden set apart in my stern counsels
Reserv'd for the days of futurity,
I have sought for a joy without pain,
For a solid without fluctuation

(*Urizen*, 4:6–11)

Murray Roston contrasts Lowth's learned primitivism with a translation of the same passage from Isaiah by a contemporary Neoclassical poet, William Langhorne:

Jehovah speaks – let all creation hear!
Thou earth attend! ye rolling Heavens give Ear!
Reared by my Care and fostered by my Hand
My rebel sons against their father stand.[2]

But there is an ambiguity on Blake's use of what is basically unrhymed anapaestic trimeter.[3] On the one hand, as Alicia Ostriker observes, 'Its greatest virtue is its power. A sense of resistless momentum appropriately informs poems dealing with a cosmic fall . . .'.[4] On the other hand, one feels that the power is harsh and stark: limited both in rhythmic subtlety and in richness of imagery and diction. This sense of limitation is also conveyed by the cramped columns into which the verse is squeezed – the columns are double, after the fashion of the printing of Bibles. The verse is infected with the limitations of the Fall it describes: its appearance on the page is that of poetry congealing into scripture.

The form of the illuminations is also imitative of their subject matter. Anne Kostelanetz Mellor, for instance, notes that 'the designs for the poem fall into | rigorously closed, tectonic forms'.[5] Furthermore, the designs are separated from the text more clearly than in almost any of Blake's illuminations hitherto, suggesting the separation of Word and Vision. And yet they are supposed to depict sublime visions.

The Book of Urizen, considered as a piece of composite art, suggests in its form the moment at which poetry (the 'Holy

Word' of the prophet-poet) solidifies into scripture, the Book of the Word (the 'Holy Word' of the 'primeval Priest'). This is also the moment when all the various arts and sciences are separated from poetry. Thus *The Book of Urizen* could be said to be hesitating between vision and limitation of vision. In an analogous way it creates uncertainty as to whether it deals with a Fall or a Creation: the Creation of the universe is seen as a Fall. And the role of Los in the latter part of the poem is ambiguous in that, though he is the prophet-poet, he seems to be necessary to the creation of Urizen's world.

These ambiguities derive, of course, from Blake's doubts about form. As usual, the doubts include his own creation of form: hence the way the book's motifs and structures waver between denoting the 'poetic' and denoting the closed or 'bounded'. But doubts about his own endeavours also surface thematically. *The Book of Urizen* could mean 'Urizen's book', in which case it would be referring to his 'Book of brass' mentioned in the poem:

> 6. Here alone I in books formd of metals
> Have written the secrets of wisdom
> The secrets of dark contemplation
> By fightings and conflicts dire,
> With terrible monsters Sin-bred:
> Which the bosoms of all inhabit;
> Seven deadly Sins of the soul.

> 7. Lo! I unfold my darkness: and on
> This rock, place with strong hand the Book
> Of eternal brass, written in my solitude.

> 8. Laws of peace, of love, of unity:
> Of pity, conpassion, forgiveness.
> Let each chuse one habitation:
> His ancient infinite mansion:
> One command, one joy, one desire,
> One curse, one weight, one measure
> One King, one God, one Law.

(4:24–40, E72/K224)

But who engraved books on copper plates? Blake. And, if *The Book of Urizen* is Urizen's book, it is also Blake's. There could be no clearer expression of his fear that he was 'imposing' and 'limiting' merely by expounding his visions.

II

Anxiety about the creation of form is also revealed by the strange role of Los in *The Book of Urizen*.

We first encounter the Los of *The Book of Urizen* when he

> round the dark globe of Urizen,
> Kept watch for Eternals to confine,
> The obscure separation alone;
> For Eternity stood wide apart
>
> (5:38–41, E73/K226)

Los attempts to heal the separation but does not succeed (7:3–4). Urizen, though 'Unorganiz'd' (6:8) and 'featureless' (7:5), is 'Rifted with direful changes' (7:6). It is true, of course, as Easson and Easson point out, that 'Los does not create these changes, despite the usual critical allegation that he does. Los only throws nets around the changes, binds the changes "with rivets of iron & brass", and forges chains for Urizen until Urizen's "eternal mind" is "locked up".'[6] Nevertheless, Los ensures that the changes are true changes, and not merely a chaotic seething. He it is who produces such form as the fallen world possesses. Another way of putting it is that, if what we see in this world is merely a reflection of 'Permanent Realities' (the Eternal Forms), to adopt Blake's later parlance ('A Vision of the Last Judgment', E555/K605), it is Los who is responsible for the fact that the fallen world reflects Eternal Forms at all. For without his activity the world of Urizen would have remained utterly inchoate. This, however, seems a poor recompense in *The Book of Urizen*: the language used to describe the form Los imposes on Urizen suggests harsh bondage and limitation. If one were to study the book in complete ignorance of the long prophecies, one would find no reason to suspect Los of being a particularly benign figure: he seems to be very much implicated in the creation of the fallen world in its harshest aspect.

One can sum up all this quite neatly by saying that Urizen causes the creation of 'bound' as limit, while Los creates true form. But we feel a certain ambivalence about Los when we read the poem – the same feeling, it is claimed, that a correct reading of the 'Introduction' to *Experience* elicits towards the Bard. Los's gift of creation is a saving grace, but he is implicated in Urizen's errors and even gives birth to the Chain of Jealousy. Blake is attempting to account for the fact that, although the Fall was a decline from Vision, it was, in fact, visionaries and poets who fell. If the creations of poets are tainted with error, how are we to regard even the loveliest forms we perceive?

Hence the ambiguity of the illuminations to *Urizen*: is this Genesis or Apocalypse? The question becomes quite pressing when we look at plate 8 (see *IB* 190). This has a design of what, from its position, could be a foetal skeleton, such as Blake might have encountered in Philip Boehmer's celebrated *Institutiones Osteologicae*.[7] From this point of view the plate emphasizes the idea of Creation as an horrific gestation. But the skull is proportionately too small for the body to be that of a foetus. Seen with this in mind the plate suggests a grisly interment in the manner of the skeleton of one who, long since buried alive, is still fixed in a cowering gesture.

In plate 6 (*IB* 188), the falling figures, wound about with serpents, may be seen as falling from Eternity into Nature. But they also recall the falling figures at the bottom of Michelangelo's *Last Judgement*, and the figure of Minos in Hell at the bottom left, wrapped around with a serpent.

But the depiction of the figure separating clouds on plate 13 (*IB* 195) and the designs of Urizen, with short hair, touching globes (pls.23, 27: *IB* 205, 209) all allude to the Creation as illustrated by Raphael in the Vatican Loggie.

In Raphael's depiction of God separating light from darkness, the deity rests his hands, with arms outstretched, on clouds to either side, as if these were solid, just as the figure in Blake's design does. Blake uses this motif to reinforce the theme of the separation of the elements of an original unity, already suggested on the title page of *Urizen* (pl.1, *IB* 183). Here Urizen holds a quill in his right hand and a burin in his left, representing the separation of Picture and Poetry, Word and Vision, and Good and Evil.

The Book of Urizen, then, wavers between two views of the Creation: from one point of view it is a disaster which produces Urizen's 'unprolific' chaos, and his neurotic and life-denying parody of form. From another point of view the disaster is mitigated by Los's creation of true form. But, since the Creation is indeed a Fall, Los's activities take on some of the repressive qualities of Urizen's. Lurking behind these conceptions is that of a cycle in which poetry declines into system, though the exigencies of writing a Creation narrative with relatively definite personages has obscured this concern. Nevertheless, *The Book of Urizen* betrays Blake's anxiety about the activity of making form in a fallen world: his ambivalent feelings are inscribed in the ambiguous form of the text and illuminations themselves.

It is worth noting that Urizen's firmness and readiness to impose are reflexes of his own weakness and internal division. For having suppressed his own energies he must be divided against himself. The title page shows Urizen attempting to write with both hands, seated in front of the cloven tablets of the Law. The cleft in the tablets descends towards the centre of Urizen's head. Blake was to become more and more interested in the idea of internal division, in 'Doubt which is Self contradiction' (*The Gates of Paradise*, E268/K770) and in 'self-imposition' (*Milton*, 7:21, E100/K487). But the line which divides the self is merely another form of 'bound'. It is just that Blake comes to believe that this internal bound is the source of all imposed bounds.

8 From *The Book of Ahania* (1795) to *Jerusalem* (1804–*c*.1820)

I

Even a work so apparently remote from political reference as *The Book of Urizen* does allude to contemporary political realities. Perhaps the best way of demonstrating this is by examining a poem that is of great interest in its own right, *The Book of Ahania*, one of two companions to *Urizen*, the other being *The Book of Los* (1795). Both share the same short-lined, metrical Bible form, with chapters and numbered verses printed in double columns. Ahania is Urizen's consort and 'female portion', and one is not surprised to learn, from the beautiful lament she is given in Chapter 5, that she is wandering far away from him. But in the first four chapters it is Urizen and Fuzon (an Orc-like figure) who dominate.

Fuzon attempts to destroy Urizen, not wishing to worship a mysterious God of wrath:

> Shall we worship this Demon of smoke,
> Said Fuzon, this abstract non-entity
> This cloudy God seated on waters
> Now seen, now obscur'd; King of sorrow?
>
> (2:10–13, E84/K249)

He throws a castrating 'Globe of wrath', thus 'The cold loins of Urizen dividing'. He imagines that he has succeeded in destroying Urizen, proclaiming proudly, 'I am God . . . eldest of things!' In usurping Urizen, he merely wishes to assume the same despotic powers, even to the extent of paradoxically claiming that he is 'eldest'. But Urizen is not dead. He smites Fuzon with a rock, and nails his corpse to the Tree of Mystery (4:5–8).

It is almost certain that these events refer to the actions and fate of Robespierre, who in June 1794 was present at a ceremony deposing the Goddess of Reason and establishing the Worship of the Supreme Being. The religious engineering is paralleled by Robespierre's political career: a libertarian turned tyrant. He himself was executed on 27 July.[1]

Urizen is the *ancien régime* in all these books, presiding over an exhausted social structure, a dead form. Orc (or Fuzon) is the spirit of revolution, always likely merely to replace one tyranny with another: 'The iron hand crushd the Tyrants head / And became a Tyrant in his stead' ('The Grey Monk', *c.*1803, E490/K419). Los represents those who continue to attempt to invest social forms with life, pointing the way towards the new order, but constantly in danger of being compromised by the old. As is said of an aspect of Los, the 'spectre of Urthona', in *Jerusalem*, 'he kept the Divine Vision in time of trouble' (44:15).

The Book of Ahania makes explicit the idea of a cycle in which Energy declines into deadly system. This had been implicit in earlier books and becomes even more explicit in later ones. Usually it involves Orc, rather than Fuzon, and Northrop Frye refers to it as 'the Orc cycle'.[2] But equally the relations of the Bard, or Los, with Urizen, suggest a cycle in which Vision declines. Indeed, the 'solidification' of Energy is not easy to distinguish from that of Vision: these faculties have distinct personifications, but the ideas they represent are closely related. In the context of *The Marriage* the 'Devourer', for instance, seems to represent one who lacks Energy. But, when one remembers Blake's attack on the Philosophy of the Five Senses, one realizes that the 'Devourer' is taking the limited world of the senses and fancying that the whole, when it has in fact been produced from the infinite perceptions of the 'Poetic or Prophetic character'. Thus the 'Producer' is both Energy and the Poetic Genius (or Vision) at the same time.

Of course, as we have seen, Los is infected with 'Jealousy' in the Lambeth books, and chains Orc. The problem for Blake is: How do either Energy or the Poetic Genius escape the limitations of the fallen world? In *The Book of Urizen* there is an oscillation between the view of form represented by Urizen and that represented by Los. In *The Book of Ahania* there is a cycle, rather than an oscillation, between Energy and repression. Thus, though Los and Orc must not be reduced to each other, Blake is finding different expressions in his myth for the idea that Energy and the Poetic Genius are closely linked, and that Urizen represents the decline of each. This idea is most succinctly expressed in 'The Mental Traveller', a lyric of *c.*1803. A 'Babe' is born, we are told, who at first is bound down by 'a Woman Old' and then 'rends up his Manacles / And binds her down for his delight' (ll.5–10, 23–4, E483–4/K424–5). In this respect he is like Orc, and she likes the Shadowy Daughter of Urthona in *America*. But then,

> He plants himself in all her Nerves
> Just as a Husbandman his mould
> And She becomes his dwelling place
> And Garden fruitful seventy fold
>
> (ll.25–8, E484/K425)

Here the youth has some of the characteristics of the redemptive Orc of *America*, but is also reminiscent of Los, in that he is a successful husbandman and gardener: that is, a creative artist.

Because of the close relationship of Energy and Vision we can at least suggest the hypothesis that Los comes between Orc and Urizen in the Orc cycle. Los is the artist torn between the life-giving claims of Energy and the need to create form, form which is always in danger of becoming the dead 'outward Ceremony' or Urizen.

II

The Book of Ahania gives a usefully succinct version of the Orc cycle. It also shows Energy in a very unflattering light. And the light remains unflattering throughout the rest of Blake's works. Indeed, in *Vala* or *The Four Zoas* (*c.*1797–*c.*1810: it is common to employ either title) one version of the myth of the Fall has it that the Fall occurred because Reason and Passion, Urizen and Luvah (Orc's unfallen form), were struggling for dominion over humanity. It's not made clear whether or not either is originally to blame. Furthermore, despite the fact that Urizen fears Orc/Luvah there is the constant suggestion that they are in alliance. Although at one point it is suggested that Luvah stole the horses of light from Urizen, at another it seems that there was some sort of agreement or exchange involved. Ahania asks Urizen,

> Why didst thou listen to the voice of Luvah that dread
> morn
> To give the immortal steeds of light to his deceitful
> hands
> No longer now obedient to thy will thou art
> compell'd
> To forge the curbs of iron & brass to build the iron
> mangers
> To feed them with intoxication from the wine presses
> of Luvah   (*Four Zoas*, 39:2–6, E326/K292)

Having given his essential energies over to Luvah, Urizen is now compelled to spur on his own activities with the perverted and sickly stimulants of fallen passion – a fact which he himself disapproves of and feels guilty about, as his response to Ahania's speech shows.

Later Urizen finds a use for Orc:

> Urizen envious brooding sat & saw the secret terror
> Flame high in pride & laugh to scorn the source of his
> deceit

> Nor knew the source of his own but thought himself
>   the Sole author
> Of all his wandering Experiments in the horrible
>   Abyss
> He knew that weakness stretches out in breadth &
>   length he knew
> That wisdom reaches high & deep & therefore he
>   made Orc
> In Serpent form compelld stretch out & up the
>   mysterious tree
> He sufferd him to Climb that he might draw all
>   human forms
> Into submission to his will nor knew the dread result
>   (80:49–51, 81:1–6, E356/K324)

This passage draws on the idea that God was somehow
testing man when he permitted the serpent to tempt Eve,
just as he was tempting Job in permitting Satan to draw
him into misfortune. In the same way, Orc can be used by
Urizen to reinforce the moral law. Indeed, he has to be used
in this way, for Urizen's law means nothing without the
existence of that which it prohibits.

Blake is beginning to see that Urizen and Orc are
entirely necessary to each other, a perception which had
always been latent in the similarity of the Satanic and
serpentine imagery used to describe both of them. He is
trying to symbolize their collusion in this poem about 'The
torments of Love & Jealousy in the Death & Judgement of
Albion the Ancient Man', as he expressed it when he
changed the title page of the *Vala* manuscript (E300/K263):
Love and Jealousy are Luvah and Urizen. Hence the new
malevolence of Orc himself:

>   Los beheld the ruddy boy
> Embracing his bright mother & beheld malignant
>   fires
> In his young eyes discerning plain that Orc plotted his
>   death
>   (60:7–9, E340/K307)

This change of attitude in Blake lends a new horror to the Orc cycle, which becomes a circle vicious at every point, rather than a way of representing the unfortunate degeneration of youthful, if misguided, Energy. In the psychology of *The Four Zoas* the Orc cycle derives from the well-established idea of the manic-depressive cycle.[3] This was conceived of as an alternation between 'Melancholy' and 'Mania'. Urizen may well be related to the aged god Saturn, who was traditionally associated with Melancholy. It is not hard to see Luvah/Orc as Mania.

The manic-depressive cycle was receiving new confirmation at the end of the eighteenth century in the empirical studies of such people as Robert James, who in his *Medicinal Dictionary* refers to observations of patients: 'melancholic patients, especially if their Disorder is inveterate, easily fall into Madness, which, when removed, the Melancholy again discovers itself, though the Madness afterwards returns at certain periods.'[4] He is insistent on the point that Mania and Melancholy are two facets of the same disorder: 'There is an absolute Necessity for reducing Melancholy and Madness to one species of Disorder . . .'[5] Melancholic patients, like Blake's 'Questioner who sits so sly' in 'Auguries of Innocence', ask 'a Reason for the most trifling and inconsistent Occurrences'.[6] The cause of the malady is 'an excessive Congestion of the Blood in the Brain'.[7] Blake is probably thinking in terms of this kind of psychology when he says that Luvah and Vala 'flew up from the Human Heart / Into the Brain' (*Four Zoas*, 10:11–12).

Blake comes to associate both Urizen and Luvah very closely with a concept he was to evolve during the period 1800–3: that of Satan the Selfhood. Each of them enters this so-called 'state' and can be redeemed from it. With this concept Blake seems to feel that he has found the cause and condition of error. He chooses to make Satan a symbol of that dead version of form which was once the distinguishing characteristic of Urizen. But he now sees 'Mathematic Form' as issuing from the division of the self between

Reason and Energy, rather than merely from a sterile version of Reason. The 'outline' moves from the circumference to the centre of a divided self. This can be seen graphically in *Illustrations of the Book of Job* (1825), where a cloud barrier frequently divides Job from the imaginary heaven into which he projects the divided state of his own soul. The Book of Job provided an especially good means of showing that it was division in itself that must be avoided, since there God and Satan collude in Job's downfall. Blake saw them as corrupt versions of Urizen and Luvah, and depicted them in accordance with his own mythology.

III

It must be about 1795, or even earlier, that Blake composed the fragment on page 141 of the *Four Zoas* manuscript, of which this is the beginning:

> Beneath the veil of Vala rose Tharmas from dewy tears
> The eternal man bowd his bright head & Urizen prince of light
> Astonishd lookd from his bright portals. Luvah king of Love
> Awakend Vala. Ariston ran forth with bright Onana
> And dark Urthona rouzd his shady bride from her deep den
> Pitying they viewd the new born demon. For they could not love
> Male formd the demon mild athletic force his shoulders spread
> And his bright feet firm as a brazen altar. but. the parts
> To love devoted. female, all astonishd stood the hosts
> Of heaven, while Tharmas with wingd speed flew to the sandy shore
>
> (Selected from the reconstruction at
> E845; see also K380)

Ariston only appears in two other places, in each case receiving only a brief mention – in *America* (10:10, E55/ K200) and in *The Song of Los* (3:4, E67/K245). Both of these are works of 1795.

This fragment is clearly a first attempt at a new myth of the Fall, in which the consorts Luvah and Vala were to have importance. Blake may have been contemplating a figure like Vala for a long time before 1795, however; H.M. Margoliouth, in his edition of *Vala*, notices the resemblance of *The Book of Thel* to the passage in Night IX of *The Four Zoas* where Vala is purified:

> Alas am I but as a flower then will I sit me down
> Then will I weep then Ill complain & sigh for
>   immortality
> And chide my maker thee O Sun that raisedst me to
>   fall
>
> So saying she sat down & wept beneath the apple trees
>
> O be thou blotted out thou Sun that raisedst me to
>   trouble
> That gavest me a heart to crave & raisedst me thy
>   phantom
> To feel thy heat & see thy light & wander here alone
> Hopeless if I am like the grass & so shall pass away
>
> Rise sluggish Soul why sitst thou here why dost thou
>   sit & weep
> Yon Sun shall wax old & decay but thou shalt ever
>   flourish
> The fruit shall ripen & fall down & the flowers
>   consume away
> But thou shalt still survive arise O dry thy dewy tears
>   (*Four Zoas*, 127:16–27, E396/K368)

Vala, unlike Thel, enters 'the pleasant gates of sleep' (128:34, E397/K369). And indeed this may reflect a previous happy ending to *Thel* itself. When Vala is redeemed she sees Luvah 'like a spirit stand in the bright air / Round him stood spirits like me who reard me a bright house' (128:35–6, E397/K369). A similar scene with Thel may, perhaps, be depicted in a sketch which never found its way into *The Book of Thel* itself.[8] Here we see a female figure, most definitely emerging from a house with arms raised and outspread: above are spirits in flight.

If the passage about Vala is indeed a reflection of an earlier ending to *Thel*, then we know roughly what was replaced by plate 6 of *Thel*, which was added to it later and now stands at the end. This is the plate in which Thel flees back to the vales of Har, afraid of the denial of self which Vala turns out to be capable of. But this pessimistic ending is also relevant to the development of Vala. The last question, in the series asked by the voice from the grave, is, 'Why a little curtain of flesh on the bed of our desire?' (6:20, E6/K130). This curtain, the hymen, can be equated with the veil of Vala: each is a limitation of Energy and Vision. Thel is horrified by this characteristic of the curtain of flesh, but acts in such a way that she will preserve it.

Which brings us back to Urizen: the hymen and the veil perform the same function as the horizon: all are types of barrier. That Blake saw Vala and Urizen as fulfilling similar functions is clear from the drawings for Young's *Night Thoughts* nos 52 and 53. No. 52 shows 'Conscience' wearing a veil and noting the sins of a dissipated drinker onto a tablet. No. 53, on the next page, shows Death (who looks exactly like Urizen) reading the sins that Conscience had indited to the 'pale Delinquent' from a book covered with incoherent blotches, like that in *Urizen*, Copy D, plate 5.[9] This implies that the sense of sin, encouraged by a belief in the separate existence of the body (Nature), is codified by Death (here the same as the recording angel, which is Urizen's role on the title page of *The Book of Urizen*).

Again, on page 27 of the *Four Zoas* manuscript there is a sketch of Urizen reclining and being enticed by a naked and merry Vala.[10] Urizen appears reluctant, perhaps partly because of Vala's teasing expression; the design, however, shows that he is in reality subordinate to the mysteries of Nature and the Female Will.

There are other similarities between the presentation of Urizen and that of Vala, as Judith Wardle has shown.[11] But it should be sufficiently clear that, in Vala, Blake has created a figure who in many respects duplicates Urizen's functions of obstructing Vision and restricting Energy. The root cause is his desire to show that the 'Gods' are in the mind of man: the usefulness of Vala was that she could be made to suggest a flaw in man's relationship with his environment: hence that other important innovation in *Vala*: 'the Ancient Man'. To have the Ancient Man as the first term of the myth seemed far less theological than to have the 'Eternals'. It also removed the impression of arbitrariness in the fall of Urizen: if man had first become subordinate to Nature it is easy to see that he might next submit to a narrow and corrupt form of Reason.

On the other hand the new solution only pushed the problem one stage further back: why should man succumb to Nature? Blake gives various differing accounts of the Fall in *Vala*, but none is conclusive.

It seems that it is impossible to identify the origin of the fall and division of the self. Blake has certain counters, representing parts of the self, and they are out of balance. But he can't say which one moved first. Indeed, the emphasis on division, rather than on the idea of one Zoa being responsible for it, indicates that Blake cannot identify the culprit. Time is fallen, one cannot go back beyond the time when division existed. This is also indicated by the all-inclusive borrowing which services Blake's myth: the Fall was and is everywhere at once. Consider a passage from *The Four Zoas*, Night III, in which Urizen tells Ahania of his fears of being usurped:

O bright [*Ahania*] a Boy is born of the dark Ocean
Whom Urizen doth serve, with Light replenishing his
    darkness
I am set here a King of trouble commanded here to
    serve
And do my ministry to those who eat of my wide table

> All this is mine yet I must serve & that Prophetic boy
> Must grow up to command his Prince
>   (38:2–7, E326/K292)

Harold Bloom correctly points out that 'The fears of Urizen
follow the pattern of Pharaoh's in Exodus 1, and Herod's in
Matthew 2, and of Zeus in the Promethean myth' (E954).
Not only that: they can be compared with the fears of the
Gnostics' evil Demiurge on discovering that Christ is to be
sent; with Saturn's fear of Jupiter; with the fears of Milton's
Satan on hearing about Messiah; and with Macbeth's fears
about Malcolm. In fact all these myths and legends are
deployed in *The Four Zoas*.

But this is bound to raise questions about Blake's
'originality', especially in his own mind.

Blake's return, as he conceived it, to the *origins* of poetry
is described in a passage already quoted from *A Descriptive
Catalogue*. He refers to his 'Apotheoses' of Nelson and Pitt as
'similar to those preserved on rude monuments, being
copies from some stupendous originals now lost'. There is a
sense then in which Blake conceives of his works as *copies of
copies*. The 'originals', though lost, are of great importance;
they connote primitive vision. And despite the ostensible
sense of the words, does there not lurk in this passage the
idea of *the copy of something lost*?

There are two copiers, or plagiarists, whom Blake can be
shown to be interested in: Macpherson and Chatterton. In
his 1826 Annotations to Wordsworth's *Poems* (1815) Blake
writes, 'I believe both Macpherson & Chatterton, that
what they say is Ancient, Is so' (E665/K783). It is at least
open to doubt whether Blake doesn't mean that Macpherson
and Chatterton are simply 'copiers' in the sense suggested
in the *Descriptive Catalogue*: that they are making something
'similar' to 'copies' of 'stupendous originals'. If you like,
they are inspired; because to be inspired in Blake's terms
means to recover an original visionary faculty. Or, again, to
be 'Ancient' (primitive) means to recover an original mode
of vision, rather than to be like this or that ancient writer or

artist. This is how Blake represents things to himself; in practice he, like Macpherson and Chatterton, is part of a web of influences.

Blake's comment about copying reveals a true anxiety that this is precisely what he's doing. And indeed he sometimes suggests that he is so dependent on his sources that he is merely a secretary. In his letter to Thomas Butts of 6 July 1803 he refers to himself as completing 'a Grand Poem. I may praise it since I dare not pretend to be other than the Secretary the Authors are in Eternity' (E730/ K825).

The effect of reading Blake's prophecies or looking at his illuminations is that of reading an endless set of quotations. Furthermore there never is any one final version of the myth of the Fall which informs his major works. At one moment Urizen is to blame, at another Vala, at another Orc/Luvah. Nevertheless the myth is trying to seem archetypal: it gestures towards a universal applicability and an 'original' structure which is everywhere shown to be impossible. There's just enough structure, or unity, in Blake's mythologies for someone to write *A Blake Dictionary*; but the alternations in meaning of key terms in different context, the digressions and inconsequentiality, put readers into a position where they are endlessly trying to read in terms of a definite structure and are endlessly involved in a process of deferred sense-making. Could it be that the 'numerous Senses' of the ancient poets, referred to in plate 11 of *The Marriage*, is an ambiguous term which refers in part to signification?

Influence, ostensible in quotation, copying and parody, is the same as structure: it is that which is known as convention and can thus be motivated. Blake's works attempt to evade subservience to influence-as-structure at the same moment as they reveal influence and structure as ineluctable: 'No doubt that by orienting and organizing the coherence of the system, the center of a structure permits the freeplay of its elements inside the total form. And even today the notion of a structure lacking any center represents

the unthinkable itself. Nevertheless, the center also closes
off the freeplay it opens up and makes possible.'[2] What
Derrida describes here is made particularly obvious in
Blake's works; and indeed it is one of their chief subjects.
Urizen, the arch-rationalist, Your Reason, who reduces
everything to unity, is precisely that 'Bad Artist', mentioned
in the Annotations to Reynolds, who 'Seems to Copy a
Great Deal' (E645/K456). The true artist copies not in a
servile sense but by putting inherited structures into play.

IV

The poet to whom Blake felt most indebted, and by whom
he felt most overshadowed, was Milton. He divined in
Milton an alienation from his 'feminine' or intuitive side,
which was neatly symbolized by his difficulties with his first
wife and his daughters. Blake brings together Milton's
three wives and three daughters as the 'Sixfold Emanation',
Ololon. But there is little to please a feminist in Blake's
analysis. Milton has been a victim of the teasing of the
Female Will:

> When the Sixfold Female percieves that Milton
> annihilates
> Himself: that seeing all his loves by her cut off: he
> leaves
> Her also: intirely abstracting himself from Female
> loves
> She shall relent in fear of death: She shall begin to give
> Her maidens to her husband: delighting in his delight
> And then & then alone begins the happy Female joy
> (*Milton*, 33:14-19, E133/K522)

He has also been the victim of his own belief in Reason. It
seems likely that the two misfortunes are linked. If Reason
is the 'bad bound', so is the wrong kind of relationship
between men and women. But the right kind of relationship
still involves the binding of women to men, one whereby
their subservience is also, mysteriously, their freedom.

Milton descends from Eternity to redeem his Sixfold Emanation, and thus also himself. The redemption occurs in Blake's garden. At dawn, as the larks are rising. Ololon appears there as a twelve-year-old girl who asks for Milton. An entity called 'Milton's Shadow' arrives, and we realize that he is the sinister side of Milton when he identifies himself as the Covering Cherub, or the Twenty-seven Churches of conventional Christianity: that is to say, the dead, outward form of the Church. Milton's Human Form arrives and denounces his Shadow (or Satan as we now realize it to be). Milton turns to Ololon, denouncing 'the Spectre; the Reasoning Power in Man', and they are reunited. (All these events occur on plates 34–43 of the poem.) Milton's self-correction implicitly justifies Blake's endeavours.

It's not entirely surprising, however, to find that Blake is equivocal in his rejection of the outward forms of Christianity:

> round [Jesus's] limbs
> The Clouds of Ololon folded as a Garment dipped in
>   blood
> Written within & without in woven letters: & the
>   Writing
> Is the Divine Revelation in the Litteral expression:
> A Garment of War, I heard it namd the Woof of Six
>   Thousand Years
>
> (42:11–15, E143/K534)

In other words the Female Will, one example of which is Ololon's separation from Milton, is responsible for the literal sense of the Bible, which is an obstruction to its inner meaning. It clothes Jesus like a garment, but this role is ambivalent: one can only reach the supposed inner core of meaning through it, but at the same time it obscures the truth. It has been constantly woven for six thousand years – the age of Earth according to Blake. Thus all the meanings that have been apparent for all of created time constitute a veil, analogous to the hymen, both bearer of, and barrier to, the supposed true meaning of history, which, according to Blake, is revealed in an instant.

That instant constitutes the implied present of *Milton*. The redemption I have described is supposed to occur instantaneously. The rest of the poem is either a delving into the fallen condition of six thousand years, or an unpacking of that supposedly instantaneous illumination. Since the instantaneous cannot provide a poem – it would have no words – Blake is forced into circumlocution. What is remarkable is how happy he is to engage in that task, to the extent of forty-five pages. Blake yearns for a unity beyond the spatial and semantic differences, and beyond the temporal deferrals, that are the condition of meaning. But, when that unity is reached, the poem stops. The artist, like 'Eternity' in Blake's proverb, is 'in love with the productions of time'. And those productions are made up of contradiction and difference: they are 'fallen', in Blake's parlance. Since it is their 'fallenness' that interests him, he sees this quality everywhere. Hence *Milton* is a very repetitive book. As Kay and Roger Easson say,

> Before the 'dull round' of time can be annihilated, it must first be recognized. This occurs in *Milton* through the static repetition of representation after representation of 'dark Satanic death', a cycle beginning with Satan, and revolving through Elynittria, Leutha, Milton's Shadow, the Sixfold Emanation, the Shadowy Female, Urizen, Rahab, Tirzah, and the virgin Ololon, returning once more to Milton's Shadow, and ending at the starting point with Satan. This cycle of error is reinforced by many graphic and verbal parallels . . .[13]

V

The same repetitiveness is apparent in Blake's last great prophetic book, *Jerusalem*.

The essential story of this poem is that Albion ('Man')

turns away from Jesus, hiding Jerusalem, his emanation, from him. The four faculties of Albion – Luvah, Urizen, Tharmas and Urthona (passion, reason, physicality and imagination) – start to war with one another. As in *The Four Zoas* and *Milton*, after the Fall Urthona becomes Los, and all these figures begin to be estranged from their emanations. Vala is Jerusalem's *shadow* in this poem. She is a sinister version of the 'feminine', and she grows powerful when Albion becomes jealous of Jerusalem. She is associated with the notions of teasing virginity, female encouragement of strife among men, and 'feminine' elusiveness. As in *The Four Zoas* she also represents the mysteriousness of Nature and the cruelty of Fate. Los is her enemy. When Albion turns from Jesus, she casts her veil over both him and Jerusalem, obscuring the vision of a better community. The effects are seen in warfare and cruelty throughout England and the world. Los labours to create Golgonooza, the imaginative city of Art, in the midst of the fallen world of Generation dominated by Vala. The symbol of that world is the forest of Entuthon Benython, which draws on associations of dark mysterious woods. But Albion falls and dies: that is, humanity becomes passive towards Nature. However, in Chapter 4 he rises again and shoots the Covering Cherub, the consolidation of evil.

But Albion falls and dies several times in the course of the poem. He gives his last words in Chapter 1: 'there Albion sunk / Down in sick pallid languor' (23:25–6). There follows a long speech, ending with the words 'Hope is banishd from me' (24:60). He dies. In Chapter 2, however, we find Albion once more capable of speech and action: 'And every Act a Crime, and Albion the punisher & judge' (28:4), But at the end of the chapter he once more utters his last words: 'There I write Albions last words. Hope is banish'd from me' (47:18). In Chapter 3 Albion is alive again, though sick at heart indeed. As in the first chapter, Albion flies from the Divine Vision and dies, though quite early on. This time the whole myth is condensed into a few lines:

> But Albion fled from the Divine Vision, with the Plow
>   of Nations enflaming
> The Living Creatures maddend and Albion fell into
>   the Furrow, and
> The Plow went over him & the Living was Plowed in
>   among the Dead
> But his Spectre rose over the starry Plow. Albion fled
>   beneath the Plow
> Till he came to the Rock of Ages. & he took his seat
>   upon the Rock.
>
> (57:12–16, E207/K689)

The living creatures are the Four Zoas, The plough is revolution, with which Chapter 3 is partly concerned, and the spectre is the 'reasoning power', with which it is also concerned.

There are many other examples of repetition in *Jerusalem*: Los's imaginative labour continues in different ways in each chapter; Vala frequently takes Jerusalem away; and the Daughters of Albion plead with Christ at the end of both Chapter 1 and Chapter 2, each time after Albion's death. The attempt to read *Jerusalem* as a single progressive narrative founders on these and other repetitions, both of main events and of more trivial ones. What was already discernible in *The Four Zoas* is here writ large: there is no archetypal pattern for this myth: it only exists in different versions.

In particular, there are four large versions for each of the four chapters of *Jerusalem*. Each chapter is addressed to a different body: the first to the Public, the second to the Jews, the third to the Deists, the fourth to the Christians. At the beginning of each is a Preface addressed to the people concerned. In each case the myth is adapted to its audience. This suggests that it may be fruitful to consider it in structuralist terms. To this task the words of Maurice Merleau-Ponty in his essay 'From Mauss to Claude Lévi-Strauss' are relevant:

> To want to understand myth as a proposition, in

terms of what it says, is to apply our own grammar and vocabulary to a foreign language. Then the whole myth has to be decoded without our even being able to postulate, as cryptographers do, that the code we are looking for has the same structure as ours. Leaving aside what myth tells us at first sight, which would tend to divert us from its true meaning, let us study its inner articulation, taking its episodes only insofar as they have what Saussure calls a diacritical value, and produce such and such a recurrent relation or contrast.[14]

Recurrent relations and contrasts in *Jerusalem* supply it with the bare bones of a structure. Thus, in Chapter 1 Albion is introduced turning away from Jesus. But in Chapter 2 he is 'the punisher & judge' associated with Old Testament morality. (28:4) and this is fitting, since the Chapter is dedicated to the Jews, whom Blake saw as the inventors of the law:

> Cold snows drifted around him: ice coverd his loins around
> He sat by Tyburns brook, and underneath his heel, shot up!
> A deadly Tree, he nam'd it Moral Virtue, and the Law
> Of God who dwells in Chaos hidden from the human sight.
>
> (28:13–16, E174/K652)

But one can only go so far with such a structuralist analysis. Many of the varied repetitions seem to be adapted to no particularly new purpose in their new context. And much of what looks like fresh narrative is simply the story of the Fall put into a new code. The story has many aspects, but not much action. It is a mistake to read *Jerusalem*, or indeed *Milton* and *The Four Zoas*, as if some obscure, coded action were being traced progressively through each line. Rather, whole paragraphs of verse will be devoted to describing, often through the speeches of the mythological *personae*, some settled aspect of the Fall. Admittedly, such descriptions are often in an obscure code, but at least one difficulty will be removed if the reader doesn't imagine that some impetuous action is going on: *Jerusalem* is a slow-moving and sometimes static allegory. When we are told that 'the Starry Heavens are fled from the mighty limbs of Albion' (75:27) we should realize that this is much the same as the statement that the 'Mundane Shell' (the 'starry floor') came into existence (59:7), the veil of the heavens that hides Eternity from us. Indeed, the Mundane Shell is also the veil of Vala (59:2–7). But the veil of Vala is also the Moral Law (21:15), the veil of the Temple (56:40) and the mortal body (55:11). Everything is fallen, everything represents the Fall. Equally significantly, almost everything is the veil of Vala. Blake sees all things as cryptic emblems of the Fall. It helps to know the Bible, it helps to have read more Blake. It helps even more to gauge the meaning of each symbol in context, and not by reference to a supposed fixed meaning. It helps to grasp the related fact that much of the poem is dramatic: consisting of monologue or dialogue of the main characters, so that the Fall is seen according to different prejudices. But most of all it helps to realize that nothing much happens in *Jerusalem*: the Fall and the fallen world are depicted in different ways, and often in the same ways. Once one has grasped this fact the poem becomes much simpler, for it really has nothing to conceal but the Fall, and when the secret is out there are no more mysteries, except perhaps why the Fall ever happened. But the causes are beyond Time, and therefore inexpressible.

Blake attacks 'Fable or Allegory' in 'A Vision of the Last Judgment' (1810, E554/K604). He wishes to criticize the use of emblems as fixed representations of ideas conceived in advance. He prefers what he calls 'Vision or Imagination', which is 'a Representation of what Eternally Exists' – that is to say, there is nothing behind the representation. But at the same time he says, 'what Critics call The Fable is Vision itself': that is to say, it is in the story and its representations, and not in some prior meaning, that 'Vision' resides. Or, to put it another way, meaning is created by the signifiers, and allegory, as commonly understood, is merely an attempt to limit and define too strictly the way in which they may be decoded.

On the other hand it is probably more helpful to think of Blake's later prophecies as allegorical rather than as 'symbolic' poems. For 'symbolism' may suggest some wealth of penumbral connotation, which Blake's prophecies lack. At times they are every bit as abstract as their bitterest critics have claimed. It is just that abstraction tends, to a generation which cherishes concrete description above all, to suggest every kind of literary dullness. In fact one may pleasurably follow, or keep learning to follow, the peculiar laws of Blake's prophecies, as long as one is willing to allow abstraction as part of the game. Since there is no ultimate myth, one is constantly engaged in a process of endlessly deferred sense-making. Consistent with this 'freeplay' is the playful wit of many of Blake's own creations. Consider, for instance, the 'Sons of Ozoth' in *Milton*:

> The Sons of Ozoth within the Optic Nerve stand fiery glowing
> And the number of his Sons is eight millions & eight.
> They give delights to the man unknown; artificial riches
> They give to scorn, & their posessors to trouble & sorrow & care,
> Shutting the sun. & moon. & stars. & trees. & clouds. & waters.
> And hills. out from the Optic Nerve & hardening it into a bone
> Opake, and like the black pebble on the enraged beach.
> While the poor indigent is like the diamond which tho cloth'd
> In rugged covering in the mine, is open all within

And in his hallowd center holds the heavens of bright
  eternity
Ozoth here builds walls of rocks against the surging
  sea
And timbers crampt with iron cramps bar in the joys
  of life
From fell destruction in the Spectrous cunning or
  rage. He Creates
The speckled Newt, the Spider & Beetle, the Rat &
  Mouse,
The Badger & Fox: they worship before his feet in
  trembling fear.   (28:29–43, E126/K515)

The illuminations are another complicating factor: they
often comment only very obliquely on the subject matter of
the text of the page they decorate. In this they function as a
visual reminder that the Fall is everywhere, while leading
one, in a very obvious way, into the process of deferred
sense-making. Although Blake conceives of his composite
art as the recovery of a lost unity of word and vision, once
more he only succeeds in stressing more emphatically the
differences and deferrals of the fallen world. It's not just
that one is struck by the difference of the subject of the
illumination from that of the text. It's also that, contrary to
the opinion of codifying critics, there's no grand system for
integrating the illuminations into a scheme where they
perform a neat, intricate and carefully planned dance with
the text.

Blake longs for a lost unity but his creations belong to
difference. The slow-moving tableaux of his later works are
the index of a political despair which sees all history as
telling one dire story, and the only way out as mental,
rather than physical, fight. But equally one should not
forget the pleasure his poems can afford, and the radical
advances in poetics they make. They avoid transcendence;
while at the same time offering a playful intellectual
manner. It seems to me that poetry has still everything to
learn from this side of Blake, stunted as it so often is at the

moment by obtuse naturalism, by suffocating certitudes, whether 'objectivist' or egotistical, and by the servitude of 'organic form'.

VI

Blake's radical Protestant background is the most decisive fact about him, even though his encounter with other traditions is an essential factor in his subtlety. It is that background which governs his complex response to the Enlightenment, a response which is, in itself, one of his chief themes. His inheritance isolated him and divided him from most other leading radicals in the literary and artistic circles where he moved – from people, that is, with whose political aims he nevertheless felt qualified sympathy. That communitarian inheritance allowed him to see through their relatively facile, Enlightenment slogans, and thus provide the most cogent poetic analysis and depiction of the forces at work in this time: his identification with the point of view of the emergent working class was enabled by that inheritance, but that identification in itself permitted him to see more clearly the history that was being made around him.

But his works also convey the sense of being divided between different discourses, with a consequent use of what Yeats, discussing his own interest in contraries ('antinomies') called 'self-distrusting methods', and a consequent ambivalence about form. Yet such self-distrust is no source of weakness in Blake. Rather the reverse. For his texts, as we have seen, make it hard for readers to establish some authoritative intention which they may feel secure about: these works provoke, question, suggest varying interpretations. Reading Blake demands a labour of interpretation. His poetry runs counter to notions of aesthetic enjoyment which have been more or less current since the middle of the eighteenth century, whereby the subject is held to perceive the work of art either in a state of perfervid intuitive empathy or in one of passive contemplation. In both accounts 'enjoyment' is conceived of as a sort of delicious residue, always left just behind the activity of actually following the work. The most important deter-minants of this view are the status of the work as an object of consumption, and the ideology of the artist–creator. On the empirical level alone this idea of enjoyment is deeply misleading about what happens when you read a poem, say. This is a practical activity, and what you 'enjoy' is inseparable from the activity of *reading the poem*.

The very manner in which Blake produced his works – as the direct product of his own craft of engraving, and in constantly changing versions – suggests a different view of art: one where the work is deprived of its status as unique, sacred expression and becomes instead the shifting, various and unstable result of processes of artistic labour.

There have been, and presumably will be, suggestions to the effect that Blake is like a modernist. And it has to be said that there is something very modern in his use of irony and ironized narrators, and something quasi-Brechtian about his provocation and questioning of the reader. On the other hand there is no hint in Blake of full-blown modernist fragmentariness. That type of modernism implies the immediate perception of essences of experience by an isolated individual, something that would make him shudder. The attempt to see Blake as a modernist poet is another type of framing, and a particularly cosy and debilitating one, for it attempts to appropriate him to a set of expectations which are seductively easy for a modern reader to deploy – though it's harder to see how they can actually work in the case of Blake. Better to see, and learn from, the way Blake goes beyond most modernist poetry in his radicalism, especially in his use of intellectual allegory and relatively abstract discourse. He is happy to use these modes because his view of humanity is thoroughly political: the individual is the bearer and mediator of traditions; the world is interpreted and transformed by those traditions. To transform the world you must institute the struggle of tradition against tradition, of discourse against discourse. This struggle is shown in Blake's works.

Notes

Chapter 1 William Blake and *Songs of Innocence*

1 Zachary Leader, *Reading Blake's Songs* (London and Boston, Mass., 1981), p.62.

2 Anne Mellor, *Blake's Human Form Divine* (Berkeley, Los Angeles and London, 1974), pp. 7, 8.

3 Roman Jakobson, 'On the verbal art of William Blake and other poet–painters', *Linguistic Enquiry*, 1 (1970), pp. 10, 9.

4 E.D. Hirsch, Jr, *Innocence and Experience: An introduction to Blake* (New Haven, Conn., and London, 1964), p. 19.

5 Isaac Watts, *Divine Songs Attempted in Easy Language for the Use of Children* (Derby, c.1840), p. 26. Reproduced in facsimile with the first edition of 1715, with an introduction and bibliography by J.H.P. Pafford (London, 1971). This song: facsimile p. 226.

6 Facsimile, ibid., p. 286.

7 Facsimile, ibid., p. 255.

8 Facsimile, ibid., p. 299.

9 Facsimile, ibid., p. 271.

10 ' "Mind-forg'd manacles" – Blake and ideology', *Red Letters*, no. 6 (n.d.), p. 17.

11 Ibid., pp. 17, 18.

12 Ibid., p. 17.

13 *The Miscellaneous Works of Hannah More* (2 vols, London, 1840), vol. II, pp. 258–9.

14 MS fragment, in William Wordsworth, *The Prelude, or Growth of a Poet's Mind*, ed. Ernest de Selincourt (Oxford, 1959), p. 571.

15 David V. Erdman, *Blake: Prophet against Empire*, 2nd edn (New York, 1969), pp. 123–4.

16 One should perhaps beware of reducing this movement of sentiment to a question of Rousseau's 'influence'.

17 This, and the preceding remark, quoted in Heather Glen, *Vision and*

Disenchantment: Blake's 'Songs' and Wordsworth's 'Lyrical Ballads' (Cambridge, 1983), p. 13.

18 Ibid.

19 Cf. the ideas of Pierre Macherey, on literature as a distorting mirror, in 'Lenin critic of Tolstoy: the image in the mirror', *A Theory of Literary Production* (London, 1978), pp. 105–35.

20 Robert Young (ed.), *Untying the Text* (Boston, Mass., London and Henley, 1981), p. 226.

21 Quoted by Young on the same page.

22 Ibid.

23 Kathleen Raine, *Blake and Tradition* (2 vols, London, 1969), vol. I, p. 22.

24 Emmanuel Swedenborg, *Concerning the Earths in our Solar System* (London, 1787), section 79. Discussed in Raine, *Blake and Tradition*, vol. I, pp. 25–6.

25 Fauvet, in *Red Letters*, no. 6, p. 39.

26 David Punter, 'Blake, Marxism and dialectic', *Literature and History*, no. 6 (Autumn 1972), p. 219.

27 Fauvet, in *Red Letters*, no. 6, pp. 24, 23.

28 Ibid., pp. 38–9. He is quoting Joseph Wicksteed, *Blake's Innocence and Experience* (London, 1928), pp. 108–9.

29 E.P. Thompson, *The Making of the English Working Class*, 2nd rev. edn (Harmondsworth, 1974), p. 34.

30 A.L. Morton, 'The Everlasting Gospel: a study in the sources of William Blake', *The Matter of Britain* (London, 1966), pp. 83–121.

31 Christopher Hill, *The World Turned Upside-Down* (Harmondsworth, 1976), ch. 14 *passim*; Keith Thomas, *Religion and the Decline of Magic: Studies in Popular Beliefs in Sixteenth and Seventeenth Century England* (London, 1971), pp. 270–1.

32 Jacques Derrida, 'Economimesis', *Diacritics*, XI, no. 2 (1981), p. 3. Derrida is talking about 'philosophy', but his remarks are equally applicable to 'art'.

Chapter 2 *Songs of Experience*

1 For a résumé of 'Tyger' criticism, see Morton Paley, *Energy and the Imagination: A Study of the Development of Blake's Thought* (Oxford, 1970), p. 39, n.2.

2 Walter Benjamin, *Illuminations* (London, 1973), p. 176.

3 Ibid., p. 174.

4 Cited ibid., p. 169.

5 Ibid. p. 168.

6 See David Simpson, *Irony and Authority in Romantic Poetry* (London, 1979), esp. pp. 89–90.

7 Urizen's pseudo-creations are like the 'Primary Qualities' of Locke, which were the mathematically measureable qualities of objects, as

opposed to the 'Secondary Qualities', such as colour, texture and smell, which he took to be inessential

8 Jonathan Culler, *The Pursuit of Signs: Semiotics, Literature, Deconstruction* (London and Henley, 1981), p. 78.

9 Ibid., p. 79.

10 Cf. Jacques Derrida, 'The white mythology: metaphor in the text of philosophy', *New Literary History*, VI, No. 1 (1974), pp. 7–74.

11 Jacques Derrida, 'Cogito and the History of Madness', *Writing and Difference* (London, 1978), p. 44.

12 Quoted by David Aers in David Aers, Jonathan Cook and David Punter, *Romanticism and Ideology: Studies in English Writing 1765–1830* (London and Henley, 1981), p. 31.

13 William Ray, *Literary Meaning: From Phenomenology to Deconstruction* (Oxford, 1984), p. 212.

14 E.P. Thompson, 'London', in *Interpreting Blake*, ed. Michael Phillips (Cambridge, 1978), p. 8.

15 Ibid.

16 Ibid., pp. 9–10.

17 Ibid., p. 10.

18 Harold Bloom, *Poetry and Repression* (New Haven, Conn., and London, 1976), p. 37.

19 Ibid., p. 42.

20 Ibid., pp. 38, 40.

21 Ibid., p. 40.

22 Ibid., p. 34.

23 Thompson, 'London', in *Interpreting Blake*, p. 13, n.12, a note which is indebted to Stan Smith.

24 Ibid., p. 13.

25 Johy Byrom, *Miscellaneous Poems* (2 vols, Manchester, 1773), vol. II, pp. 306, 307.

26 See Paley, *Energy and the Imagination*.

Chapter 3 Unsteady States:|*Songs of Innocence and of Experience*

1 Robert F. Gleckner, 'Point of view of context in Blake's songs', *Bulletin of the New York Public Library*, LXI, no. 11 (Nov 1957), p. 535.

2 See M.H. Abrams, *The Mirror and the Lamp: Romantic Theory and the Critical Tradition* (London, Oxford, New York, 1953), pp. 78–84.

Chapter 4 The Ambiguity of Bound: *'There is No Natural Religion'* (c.**1788**), *Europe* **(1794)**

1 Voltaire, *A Treatise on Religious Toleration* (London, 1764), pp. 244–5.

2 Ernst Cassirer, *The Philosophy of the Enlightenment*, tr. F.C.A. Koelln and J.P. Pettegrove (Princeton, NJ, 1951), p. 23.

3 Cf. 'Annotations to Reynolds' (E659/K475): Blake uses nearly the

same words to reply to the soundly Neoclassical premise of taste: 'We will take it for granted, that reason is something invariable and fixed in the nature of things.'

4 'Vortexes', not vortices, are discussed on pp. 88ff.; particles ('little balls') of light, pp. 41–2; inhabitants of the moon, pp. 40–71; microscopic life: 'A mulberry leaf is a little world, inhabited by multitudes of these invisible worms, which, to them, is a country of vast extent' (p. 76); 'fancy then millions of creatures to subsist many years on a grain of sand' (p. 77). All these ideas find echoes in Blake's work.

5 Mary Wollstonecraft, *Original Stories from Real Life*, 2nd edn (London, 1791), pp. iv–v; emphasis added.

6 J.J. Rousseau, *Emilius and Sophia; Or, A New System of Education*, tr. W. Kenrick (4 vols, London, 1783), vol. II, p. 51.

7 Quoted in Cassirer, *The Philosophy of the Enlightenment*, p. 73.

8 Gerd Buchdahl, *The Image of Newton and Locke in the Age of Reason* (London and New York, 1961), p. 2.

9 Donald Ault, *Visionary Physics* (Chicago, 1974), p. 78; Isaac Newton, *Mathematical Principles of Natural Philosophy*, tr. Robert Thorp (London, 1777), Vol. I (no more published), pp. 53, 72, 73.

10 *The European Fame of Isaac Newton*, catalogue of an exhibition in the Fitzwilliam Museum, University of Cambridge, 22 Nov. 1973 – 6 Jan. 1974 [?Cambridge, ?1973], editor(s) unnamed, commentary pp. 4–7.

11 Voltaire, *Elements of Sir Isaac Newton's Philosophy*, tr. J. Hanna (London, 1783), p.v.

12 [J.J.] Winckelmann, *Reflections on the Painting and Sculpture of the Greeks*, tr. Henry Fuseli (London, 1765), p. 22.

13 Plotinus, *An Essay on the Beautiful* [tr. Thomas Taylor] (London, 1792, p. ix.

14 R.T. Wallis, *Neoplatonism* (London, 1972), p. 6.

15 Ibid., p. 57.

16 *Five Books of Plotinus*, tr. Thomas Taylor (London, 1794), p. 240; and *On the Beautiful*, pp. 42–3.

17 Walter Pater, *The Renaissance* (New York, 1959), pp. 139–40.

18 Julia Kristeva, 'Signifying practice and mode of production', *Edinburgh Magazine*, no. 1 (n.d.), p. 64.

19 Edward Larrissy, 'Blake's *America*: an early version?', *Notes and Queries*, n.s., XXX, no. 3 (June, 1963), pp. 217–19.

20 Jacques Derrida, 'Structure, sign and play in the discourse of the human sciences', *The Structuralist Controversy*, ed. Richard Macksey and Eugenio Donato (Baltimore and London, 1972), p. 248.

Chapter 5 ¡*The Marriage of Heaven and Hell*' (*c*.**1791–3**)

1 For instance by Graham Pechey, '*The Marriage of Heaven and Hell*: a

text and its conjuncture', *Oxford Literary Review*, III, no. 3 (Spring, 1979), pp. 52–98.

2 Emmanuel Swedenborg, *A Treatise concerning Heaven and Hell, and of the Wonderful Things Therein* (London, 1784), p. 14.

3 [George Larkin], *The Visions of John Bunyan* [Leeds, c.1750], pp. 16, 22–36.

4 Swedenborg, *Treatise*, p. 143.

5 *Russian Formalist Criticism: Four Essays*, ed. Lee T. Lemon and Marion J. Reis (Lincoln, Nebr., 1965), p. 80.

6 Roland Barthes, *S/Z*, tr. Richard Miller, preface by Richard Howard (London, 1975), p. 206.

7 Ibid.

8 Jonathan Culler, *Structuralist Poetics* (London, 1975), p. 158.

9 Friedrich Schlegel, 'Athenäum-Fragmente', *Kritische Schriften* (Munich, 1970), p. 31.

10 Anne K. Mellor, *English Romantic Irony* (Cambridge, Mass., and London, 1980), pp. 23–4.

Chapter 6 Usurpation and Confusion of Powers

1 '. . . for to display the different Effects of Liberty and Tyranny, is the chief design of his *Paradise Lost*' – John Toland, *The Life of John Milton*, in *The Early Lives of Milton*, ed. Helen Darbishire (London, 1932), p. 182.

2 Reproduced in *William Blake*, catalogue of the Tate exhibition (London, 1978) no. 90.

3 David Wagenknecht, *Blake's Night: William Blake and the Idea of Pastoral* (Cambridge, Mass., 1973), pp. 295–6.

4 Paley, *Energy and the Imagination*, pp. 1–29.

5 Pechey, in *Oxford Literary Review*, III, no. 3., p. 53.

6 Anon., *The World Turn'd Upside-Down*, eighteenth-century broadside (n.d.).

7 *The Notebook of William Blake: A Photographic and Typographic Facsimile*, ed. David V. Erdman (Oxford, 1973), pp. 47–8.

8 John Beer, *Blake's Humanism* (Manchester, 1968), p. 24.

9 Helen Gardner, *A Reading of Paradise Lost* (Oxford, 1965), p. 119.

10 Ibid.

11 Emmanuel Swedenborg, *A Treatise concerning Heaven and Hell* (London, 1778), p. 372.

12 Erdman, *Notebook*, facing Notebook p. 110.

13 There is no evidence for the date (c.1797–1800) assigned to the Notebook poem 'When Klopstock England defied' by Erdman (*Notebook* pp. 6, 12). There are good reasons for agreeing with Keynes's dating of c.1793 (K186–7).

14 Friedrich Klopstock, *The Messiah* (London, 1763), p. 10.

15 See Larrissy, in *Notes and Queries*, n.s., XXX, no. 3.

16 Leopold Damrosch, Jr, *Symbol and Truth in Blake's Myth* (Princeton, NJ), p. 197.
17 Jacques Derrida, 'The double session', *Dissemination*, tr. Barbara Johnson (Chicago, 1981), pp. 173–285; Maud Ellmann, 'Floating the Pound: the circulation of the subject of the *Cantos*', *Oxford Literary Review*, III, no. 3 (Spring, 1979).
18 Ibid, p. 25.

Chapter 7 *The Book of Urizen* **(1794)**

1 Robert Lowth, *Isaiah: A New Translation* (London, 1791), p. 95.
2 Quoted in Murray Roston, *Prophet and Poet* (London, 1965), p. 136.
3 See Alicia Ostriker, *Vision and Verse in William Blake* (Madison and Milwaukee, 1965), p. 164. Not, as Harold Bloom thinks, 'a four-beat verse' – *Blake's Apocalypse* (London, 1963), p. 164 – though the poem occasionally slips into tetrameter.
4 Ostriker, *Vision and Verse*, p. 165.
5 Mellor, *Blake's Human Form Divine*, p. 89.
6 *William Blake: The Book of Urizen*, ed. Kay Parkhurst Easson and Roger R. Easson (London, 1979), p. 76.
7 Philip Boehmer, *Institutiones Osteologicae* (Magdeburg, 1749).

Chapter 8 From *The Book of Ahania* **(1795) to** *Jerusalem* **1804–c.1820)**

1 Erdman, *Prophet against Empire*, pp. 314–15.
2 Northrop Frye, *Fearful Symmetry: A Study of William Blake* (Princeton, NJ, 1947), pp. 207–35.
3 Michel Foucault, *Madness and Civilization*, tr. Richard Howard (London, 1977), p. 131, and pp. 117–35 in general.
4 Robert James, *A Medicinal Dictionary* (3 vols. London, 1743–5), vol. II, article on 'Mania' (unpaginated).
5 Ibid.
6 Ibid.
7 Ibid.
8 Two sketches for *The Book of Thel*, c.1789 (private collection), reproduced in *William Blake*, Tate catalogue, no. 49.
9 The many watercolour drawings for *Night Thoughts* were transformed into engravings to go around the text of that work published by Richard Edwards (London, 1797): only the first four Nights were published. See *William Blake's Designs for Edward Young's Night Thoughts*, ed. D. Erdman, J. Grant, E. Rose and M. Tolley (Oxford, 1980).
10 William Blake, 'The Four Zoas' (1797 [–1808?]), British Library Add. MS 39764. The whole MS is reproduced in photographic facsimile in *Vala, or the Four Zoas*, ed. G.E. Bentley, Jr (Oxford, 1963).

11 Judith Wardle, 'Blake and iconography: analogues of Urizen and Vala', *Colby Library Quarterly*, XIV, no. 3 (Sep. 1973), pp. 125–65.
12 Macksey and Donato, *The Structuralist Controversy*, p. 248.
13 *William Blake: Milton*, ed. Kay Parkhurst Easson and Roger R. Easson (London, 1979), p. 141.
14 Maurice Merleau-Ponty, *Signs* (Evanston, Ill., 1964), p. 121.

Index